# Do-It-Yourself

Includes online audio, instructional video & downloadable fingering chart

# CLARINET

BY MICHELLE ANDERSON
AND DEBORAH ANDRUS

To access audio and video, visit:
**www.halleonard.com/mylibrary**

Enter Code
1664-5363-5735-8479

ISBN 978-1-7051-4124-3

A Muse Group Company



Visit Hal Leonard Online at
**www.halleonard.com**

World headquarters, contact:
**Hal Leonard**
7777 West Bluemound Road
Milwaukee, WI 53213
Email: info@halleonard.com

In Europe, contact:
**Hal Leonard Europe Limited**
Dettingen Way
Bury St Edmunds, Suffolk, IP33 3YB
Email: info@halleonardeurope.com

In Australia, contact:
**Hal Leonard Australia Pty. Ltd.**
4 Lentara Court
Cheltenham, Victoria, 3192 Australia
Email: info@halleonard.com.au

# ABOUT THE AUTHORS

**Michelle Anderson** is a professional clarinetist and teacher who lives in Vancouver, British Columbia, and teaches clarinet at the University of British Columbia School of Music. She performs regularly with various professional orchestras and loves to play chamber music with the ensemble Trio Harmonie. She is in demand as a guest teacher and soloist at clarinet festivals around the world. Michelle is the Founder of Clarinet Mentors (www.ClarinetMastery.com), one of the largest online clarinet educational resources. Michelle enjoys teaching adult clarinetists from all over the world through her online masterclasses, courses, and special live events. She has a mission to make clarinet fun and easy for people worldwide. As of this printing, the Clarinet Mentors YouTube channel has been viewed more than 3.8 million times.

Equal parts entrepreneur, educator, and clarinetist **Deborah Andrus** has been lauded for her "inspirational teaching." Her award-winning clarinet students hail from locations around the world, including China, Great Britain, Australia, Canada, and the United States. Dr. Andrus connects with her students through in-person and online lessons and masterclasses through her company, Clarinet Guide, for Clarinet Mentors, and as the Clarinet Teaching Artist at Lehigh University since 2004.

Dr. Andrus is a member of the Allentown Symphony Orchestra, the SATORI Chamber Ensemble, and the DeMarina Trio. Deborah wrote the clarinet chapters in *Teaching Woodwinds* (Mountain Peak Music 2014/2020), a resource for music educators. Her book *The Chalumeau Register* was released in 2020.

**Marilyn Fleming** is a retired computer entrepreneur. She made first chair clarinet at All-State in high school, continued to play a bit in college, and then put the instrument away in a closet while pursuing a different career path. Returning to the clarinet in her retirement years, she's approaching clarinet education from a student's perspective. Marilyn is fascinated by the use of technology, particularly the use of computers and recording equipment to turbo-charge practice sessions. She studies online with Dr. Andrus, performs regularly on Facebook groups, and has served as a quality assurance advisor for a music practice app. She is the co-author with Deborah Andrus of the book *The Chalumeau Register*.

# ACKNOWLEDGMENTS

*Do-It-Yourself Clarinet* features music from many talented composers over the past few centuries. We are fortunate to share their music with you in this collection of pieces. We owe a huge debt of gratitude to Marilyn Fleming, a clarinetist and computer whiz, who spent countless hours (or higher than we can count) organizing several hundred files of text, pictures, figures, and musical examples in producing this book. We could not have completed it without her wisdom, skill, and patient guidance. Special thanks to clarinet virtuoso and photographer Jose Franch-Ballester, who took the photos for our Clarinet Fingerings Chart, and to videographer and photographer Joshua Kovar from Lehigh University's Zoellner Arts Center. We also appreciate the contributions of clarinetist Sasko Temelkoski, who translated many of our hand-written exercises into electronic format for this publication. Thanks to clarinetist Aaron McDonald for his help with proofreading and his insightful suggestions. We give special thanks to our editor Brittany McCorriston at Hal Leonard for her patience and vision in helping to bring this book to life.

As always in a project this big, we thank our families for their patience as the authors toiled over B-flat or B-naturals into the wee hours of the morning. This book would not be possible without the inspiration from all our amazing clarinet students over the years, including children and adults of all levels of experience. We are all united in our love of music and our desire to play this music more easily on our clarinets, and *Do-It-Yourself Clarinet* is intended to aid in that mission.

# CONTENTS

**ABOUT THE AUTHORS** .......... 2
**ACKNOWLEDGMENTS** .......... 3
**INTRODUCTION** .......... 6
**LESSON 1:** First Notes .......... 17
**LESSON 2:** Eighth Notes .......... 23
**LESSON 3:** Accidentals and Key Signatures .......... 28
**LESSON 4:** Building Our Musical Vocabulary .......... 32
**LESSON 5:** Chromatics and Enharmonics .......... 43
**LESSON 6:** Sixteenth Notes .......... 50
**LESSON 7:** Triplets .......... 60
**LESSON 8:** Putting It All Together .......... 66
**LESSON 9:** The Clarion Register .......... 72
**LESSON 10:** Connecting the Registers .......... 80
**LESSON 11:** Tempo Changes .......... 91
**LESSON 12:** The Upper Clarion Register .......... 108
**LESSON 13:** The Altissimo Register .......... 118
**LESSON 14:** Continuing Your Journey .......... 133
**APPENDIX A:** Vocabulary Terms .......... 146
**APPENDIX B:** Clarinet Fingerings .......... 147

# SONG INDEX

Addams Family Theme .......... 60
Ain't Misbehavin' .......... 104
Air on a G String (Duet) .......... 116
All Join Hands .......... 69
All You Need Is Love (Duet) .......... 58
Alouette .......... 54
America .......... 141
Andante Grazioso (Duet) .......... 90
Anti-Hero .......... 85
The Ants Go Marching In .......... 126
Are You Lonesome Tonight? .......... 98
Arirang .......... 35
Ashokan Farewell .......... 135
Au Clair de la Lune .......... 21
Baby Elephant Walk .......... 137
Baby Shark .......... 34
Bad Romance .......... 39
Batman Theme .......... 44
Beauty and the Beast .......... 91
Bibbidi-Bobbidi-Boo (The Magic Song) .......... 103
Blackbird .......... 26
Bound for South Australia .......... 111
Bridge Over Troubled Water .......... 82
Bye Bye Love .......... 76
Cantina Band .......... 114
The Clarinet from the Orchestra Song .......... 27
Come Sail Away .......... 75
Dance Monkey .......... 77
Danny Boy .......... 134
Dawn .......... 57
Deep River Blues .......... 56
Detroit City .......... 113
Do-Re-Mi .......... 45
Downtown .......... 76
A Dream Is a Wish Your Heart Makes .......... 89
Easy on Me .......... 57
Edelweiss .......... 84
Eight Days a Week .......... 110
Eleanor Rigby .......... 112
Every Breath You Take .......... 25
Fais Do-Do (Go to Sleep) .......... 73
Finale (Duet) .......... 70
Firework .......... 77

Follow the Yellow Brick Road/We're Off to See the Wizard ... 125
Frère Jacques (Are You Sleeping?) ... 30
The Galway Piper ... 50
Glimpse of Us ... 128
Habanera ... 61
Hanukkah, O Hanukkah ... 124
Happy Birthday to You ... 56
A Hard Day's Night ... 61
He's Got the Whole World in His Hands ... 109
Hey Jude ... 55
Hot Cross Buns ... 21
I Say a Little Prayer ... 136
In the Good Ole Summertime ... 120
Itsy Bitsy Teenie Weenie Yellow Polka Dot Bikini ... 92
James Bond Theme ... 63
Theme from "Jaws" ... 51
Jingle Bells ... 33
Joy to the World ... 34
Theme from "Jurassic Park" ... 83
Karma Chameleon ... 69
Klezmer Contra ... 68
La Fille Aux Cheveux De Lin (The Girl with the Flaxen Hair) ... 140
Lean On Me (Duet) ... 42
Leaving of Liverpool ... 82
Let's Go Fly a Kite ... 123
Liberty Bell March ... 129
Lift Me Up ... 86
Linus and Lucy (Duet) ... 78
The Lion Sleeps Tonight ... 111
London Bridge ... 36
Love Me Do ... 26
Love Me Tender ... 30, 109
Made You Look ... 47
Make New Friends ... 84
Mamma Mia ... 25
Mary and Martha ... 74
Merrily We Roll Along ... 21
Mission: Impossible Theme ... 139
Moonlight Serenade ... 142
The Mulberry Bush ... 125
The Music of the Night ... 97
My Bonnie Lies Over the Ocean ... 122
My Dreidel ... 46
My Favorite Things ... 100
My Heart Will Go On (Love Theme From 'Titanic') ... 33
Norwegian Wood (This Bird Has Flown) ... 127
Nowhere Man ... 88
Ob-La-Di, Ob-La-Da ... 87
Ode to Joy ... 32, 74
One Call Away ... 77
Over the Rainbow (Duet) ... 48
Part of Your World ... 46
Perfect ... 128
Piano Man ... 101
Pick-A-Little, Talk-A-Little/ Goodnight Ladies ... 93
Pink Panther (Duet) ... 64
Rock Around the Clock ... 99
Rondo (Duet) ... 130
Row, Row, Row Your Boat ... 54
Shallow ... 40
Sharper Hot Cross Buns ... 29
Shenandoah ... 121
Shepherd's Hey ... 83
Simple Gifts (Duet) ... 27
The Sleigh Ride ... 37
Spring (Duet) ... 31
Star Wars (Main Theme) ... 67
Stormy Weather (Keeps Rainin' All the Time) ... 105
Stranger on the Shore ... 115
The Stripper ... 102
Supercalifragilisticexpialidocious ... 63
Take Five ... 138
Tequila ... 39
Three for Two (Duet) ... 22
Tideo ... 67
Turn! Turn! Turn! (To Everything There is a Season) ... 75
We Are the Champions ... 126
We Will Rock You ... 24
What a Wonderful World (Duet) ... 143
What the World Needs Now Is Love ... 41
When I'm Sixty-Four (Duet) ... 106
When the Saints Go Marching In ... 94
Whistle While You Work ... 96
Wipe Out ... 45
Y.M.C.A. ... 38
Yakety Yak ... 112
Yesterday ... 92
You Belong with Me ... 95

# INTRODUCTION

Welcome to *Do-It-Yourself Clarinet*! Whether you are a new clarinetist or returning after a long break, you will find clear direction here on the best habits to play the clarinet. Our goal is to get you playing music that you know and love as quickly as possible. At the same time, you will be developing proper techniques to sound good as you perform. Videos to support your learning are also included.

This book is divided into 14 lessons, with each introducing new musical and technical concepts. There are clapping exercises to help you learn rhythm and music reading, with a video for each that reviews those exercises. Every lesson ends with a play-along duet. You can listen to the performance, as well as each part separately, so that you can play along with us. As each new note is introduced, we show the fingerings in a standard clarinet fingering chart format. A fingering chart with photographs of each fingering is also included as a downloadable PDF (see "Online Resources" for how to access it). You'll also see lots of short finger exercises (called Loopy Loops) that are designed to help you learn fingerings until they feel automatic. Building these skills will help you play clarinet well as you join us in a fun and progressive musical journey. Finally, we've chosen a variety of tunes that represent many musical styles for you to enjoy. It's time to begin your clarinet journey!
–Michelle Anderson & Deborah Andrus

## Online Resources

On page 1, you will find a unique code. Go to **www.halleonard.com/mylibrary** and enter the code to gain access to the audio, video, scale guide, and clarinet fingering chart for download or streaming. There, you will find expert video instruction to get you started with the best habits for success, plus audio demonstrations of many songs found in this book. These lessons are indicated throughout the book by these symbols:

Also included is ***PLAYBACK+***, a multi-functional audio player that allows you to slow down audio without changing pitch, set loop points, and pan left or right—available exclusively from Hal Leonard.

## Parts of the Clarinet

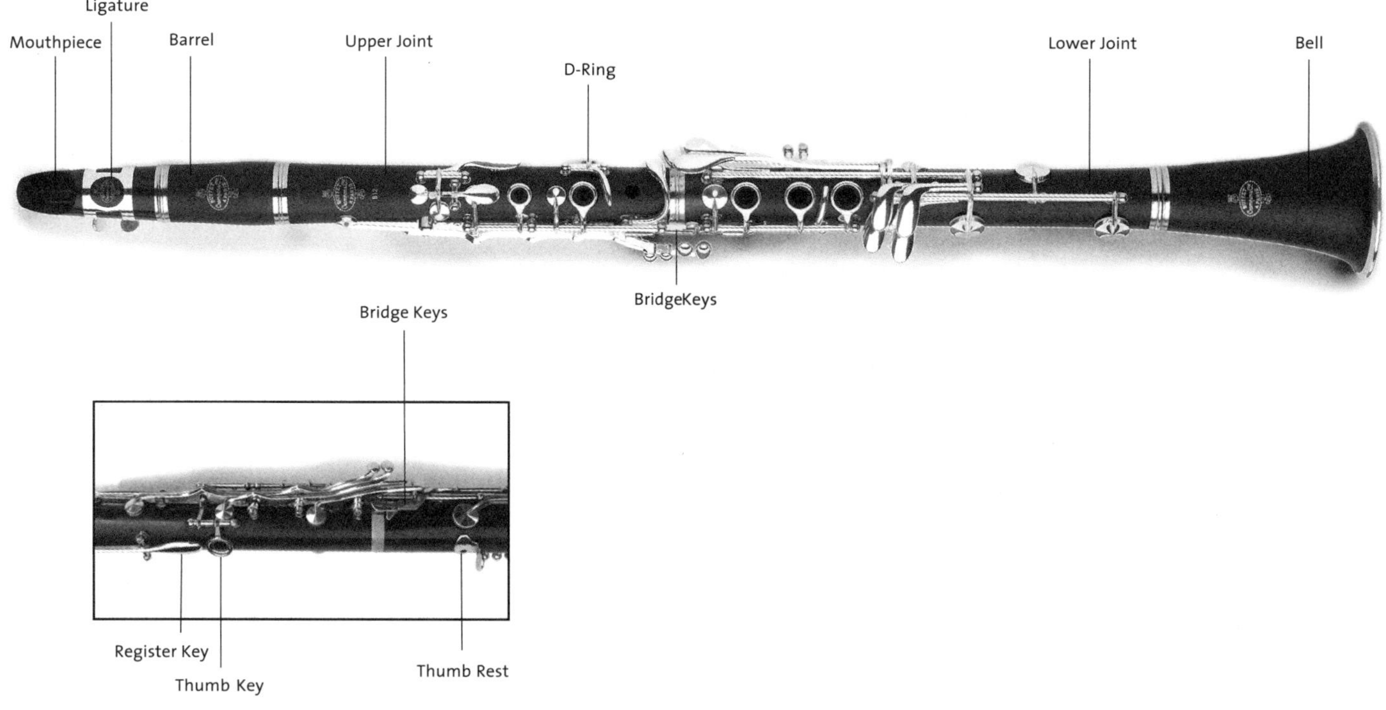

# Assembling the Clarinet

*To access online resources, head over to* ***www.halleonard.com/mylibrary*** *and input the code found on page 1!*

When opening your case, hold it securely on your lap or place it on the floor. Ensure that it is upright, the handle is on the bottom, and the logo is on the top.

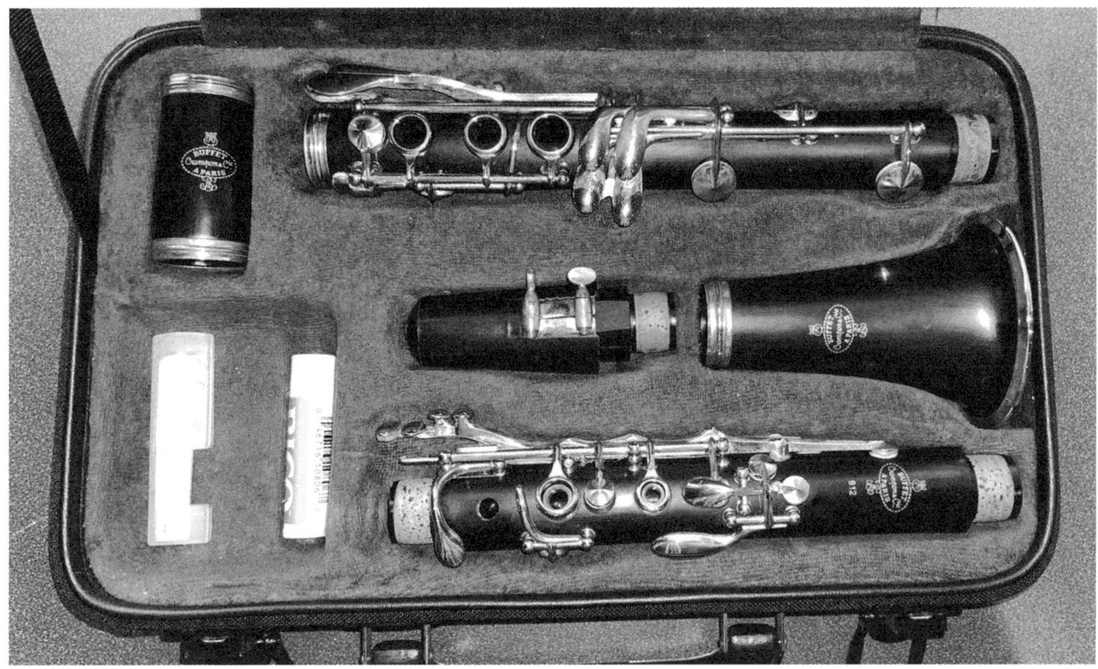

To assemble the clarinet, we'll start with the reed. Remove the reed from the reed case, ensure it is clean and undamaged (no chips!), and place the thin portion in your mouth to moisten it.

Then, take your cork grease and put a very thin layer on each of the corks. Gently rub the cork grease into each of the corks on the bottom joint, top joint, and mouthpiece.

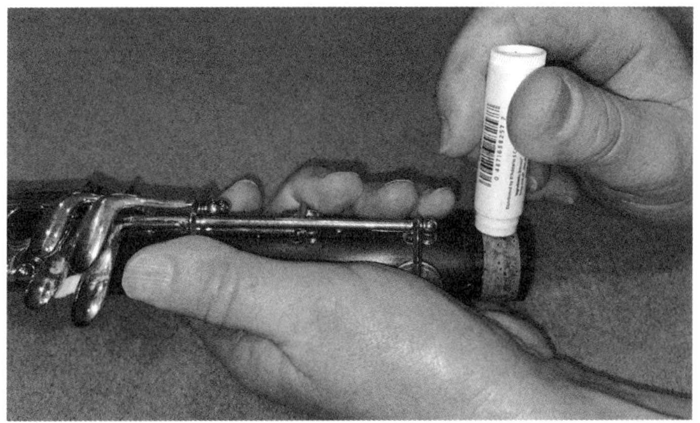

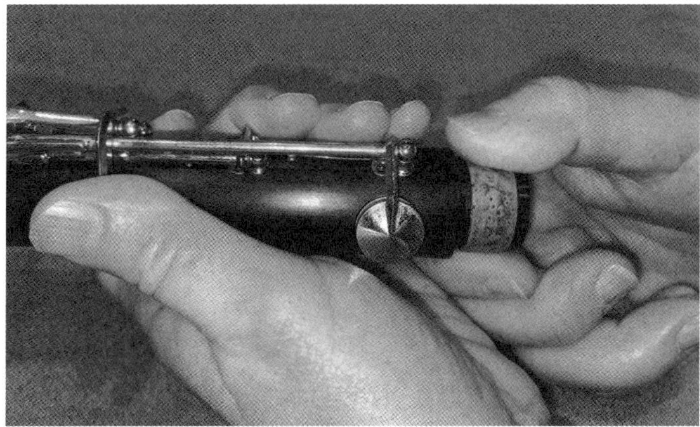

Take your bell and gently twist it onto the lower joint.

Lift out the upper joint, and make sure your bridge key is facing downward. To raise the bridge key, close your fingers over the D-ring. Line up the bridge on the top joint with the bridge on the lower joint. Gently twist the upper and lower joints together using the bridge key connection to check the alignment of the two joints. Keep the D-ring bridge key raised until the two joints are connected.

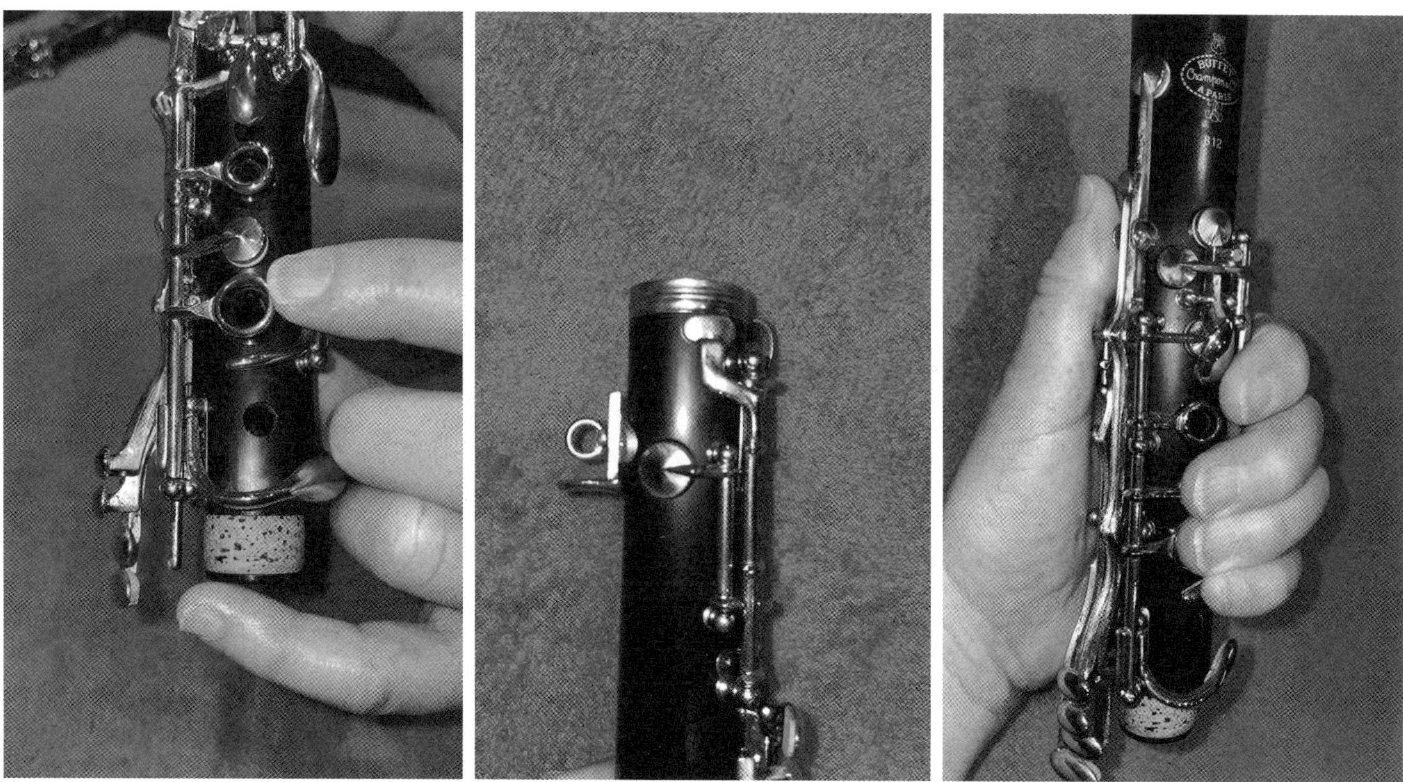

Hold the upper joint and twist the barrel on. Next, twist on the mouthpiece so the window portion aligns with the thumb hole and the register key.

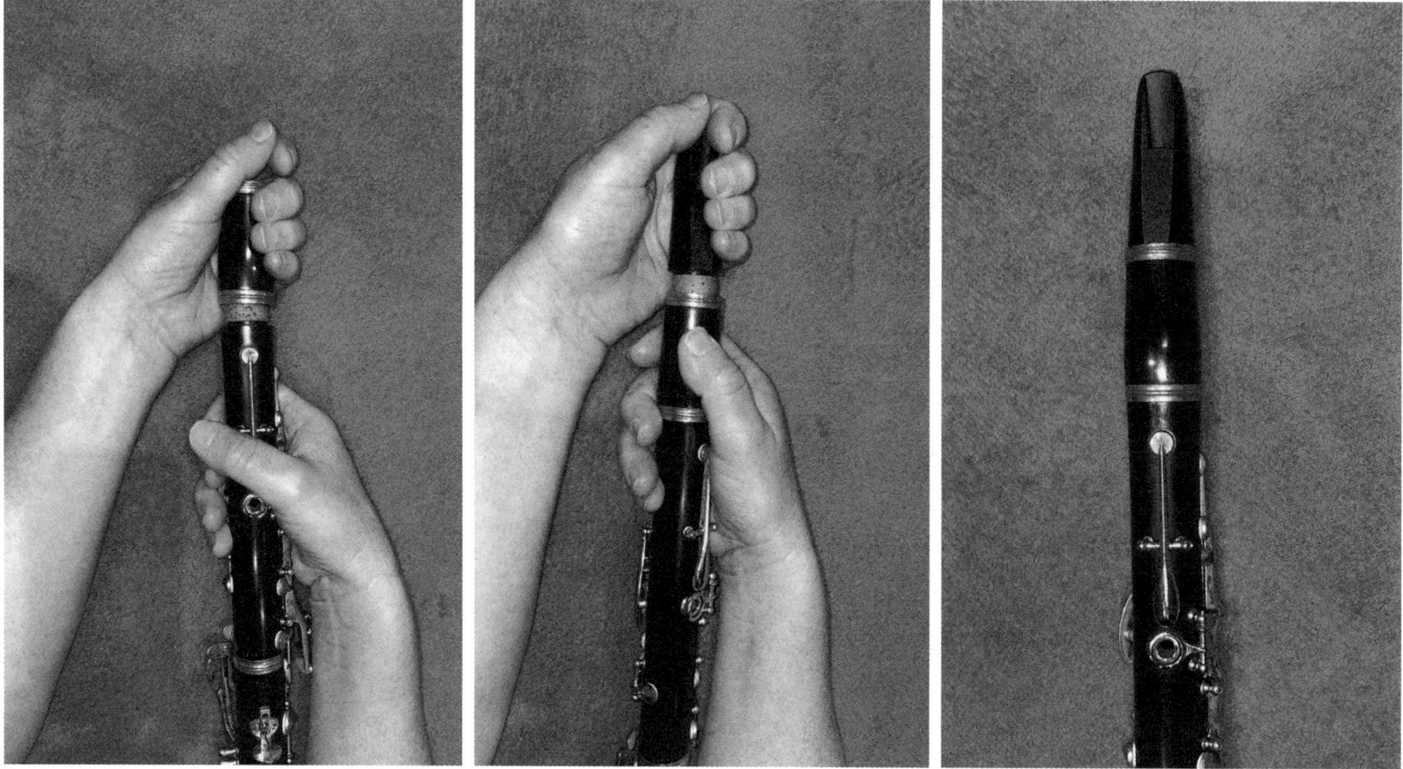

## Adding the Reed to the Mouthpiece

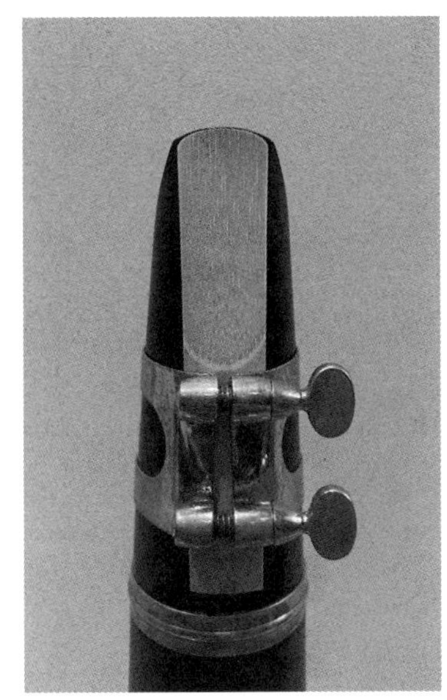

1. With your clarinet fully assembled, rest the bell on your knee and face the keys forward. The window of the mouthpiece should be facing you.
2. Align the reed with the thin portion upright and the thicker portion beneath. The reed should be even with the top of the mouthpiece.
3. Carefully slide the ligature over the reed. Make sure that the ligature screw(s) are toward your right as you look at the reed. Align the top of the ligature with the lines on your mouthpiece (or just under where the cut portion of the reed ends and the bark starts).
4. Tighten the ligature screw(s) so that the ligature holds the reed securely in place on the bark portion of the reed. If using a synthetic reed, experiment with how tightly you clamp down with the screws. Generally, synthetic reeds respond better with a firmer attachment than cane reeds.

CLARINET TALK

**Cane vs. Synthetic Reeds**

The clarinet makes sound by the vibration of the reed against the mouthpiece as we blow fast air across it. Traditionally, clarinet reeds have been made from cane (similar to bamboo) and must be moist to vibrate properly. Recently, many good synthetic reeds have been developed by leading reed manufacturers. Synthetic reeds are much more durable and less sensitive to changes in humidity. However, they are more expensive, and some brands do not produce as warm of a tone as traditional cane. As of this publication, most professional players still use cane, but many are switching to synthetic as the technology improves. The authors use synthetic reeds.

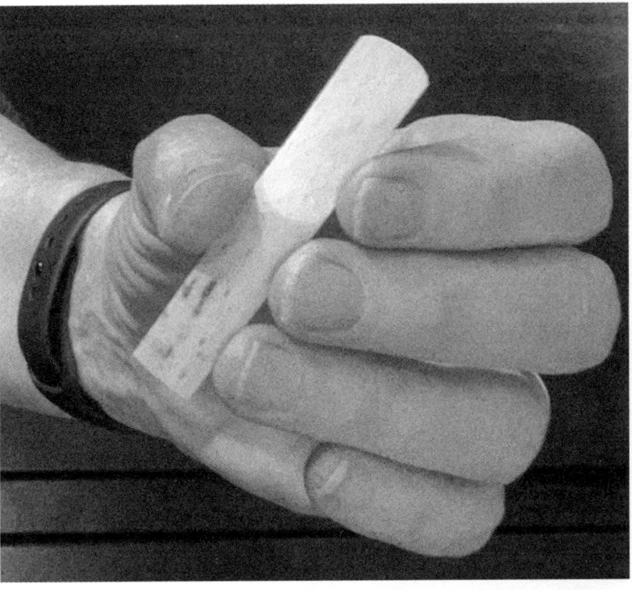

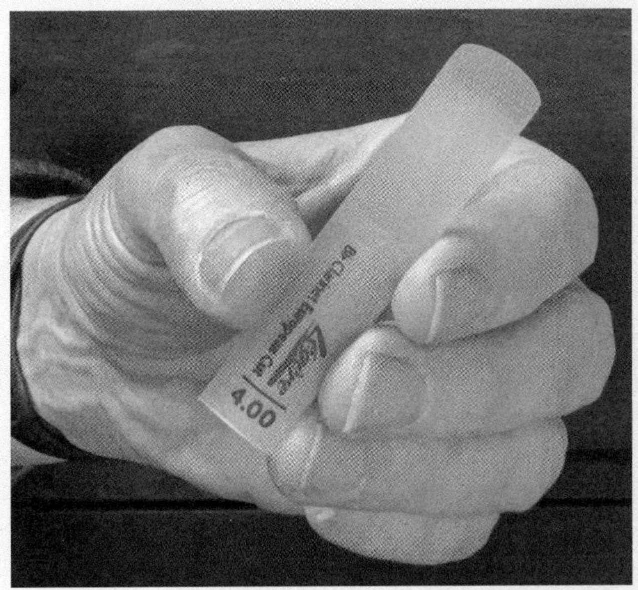


| **Cane** | **Synthetic** |
|---|---|
| Pros: Less expensive; good ones help produce great tone. As a beginner, you may outgrow your size quickly, so you may want to wait to invest in a synthetic reed until you stabilize a bit.<br>Cons: Less durable; they warp/change with the weather and have inconsistent quality out of the box. | Pros: Very stable and durable (play well for months as opposed to weeks); good ones help produce great tone. More consistent out of the box.<br>Cons: More expensive; some mouthpieces work better than others with synthetic reeds. Long-time cane users often need to adjust to these to sound good. |

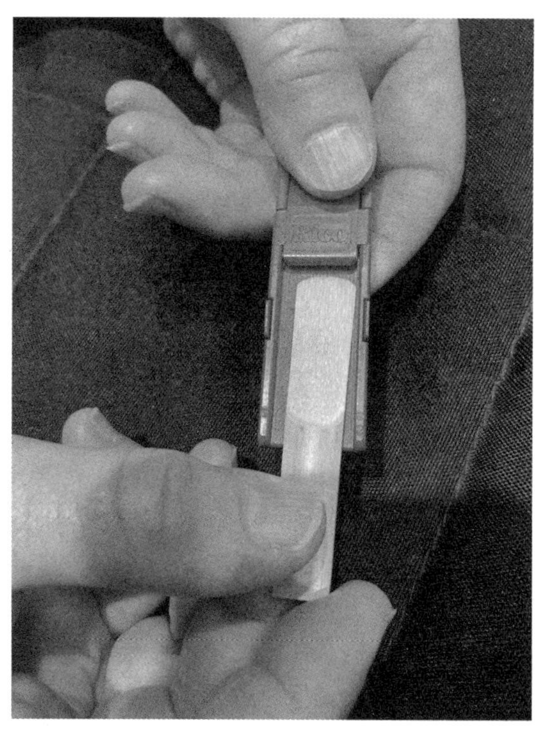

## Cleaning

When finished playing, remove the reed from the mouthpiece and slide it back into the protective case with the back of the reed toward the flat portion of the reed case. Pay careful attention to protect the thin tip of the reed.

Remove the ligature and place it inside the cap. Hold the barrel and remove the mouthpiece. Pull the swab through the mouthpiece from the bottom (the cork) to the top (the beak).

With the rest of the clarinet still assembled, drop the weighted end of the swab into the bell and pull it through at the barrel (from the bottom of the clarinet to the top). Repeat two to three times to remove most of the moisture. Disassemble the clarinet from barrel to bell, cleaning out the tenons with the swab once more.

Be sure to clean your clarinet after each playing session. When the swab is dirty, it can be washed by hand or in a washing machine and then hung up to air dry.

# Holding the Clarinet

## Right Hand Position

Pretend you are shaking hands with someone in front of you. Notice that your right thumb and thumbnail face upward, and the inside of your fingers face left in a relaxed curve.

Slide the inside of the right thumb (the portion that is closest to the index finger) up the back of the clarinet until the knuckle reaches the thumb rest. The weight of the clarinet rests on your right thumb knuckle.

The right fingers float over the three tone holes on the front of the instrument, and the pinky floats over the F/C key.

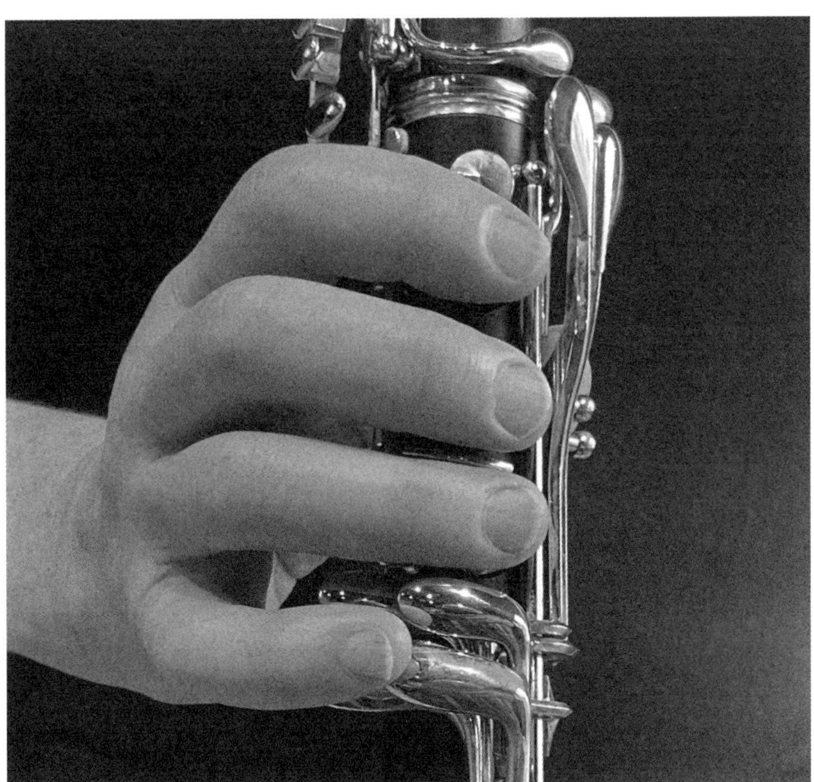

## Left Hand Position

The pad of the left thumb covers the thumb hole while simultaneously touching the register key. The tip of your thumb should gently rest on the register key without pressing it. The thumb points upward and slightly to the right. The left wrist is also in a neutral position. The fingers curve naturally from the back knuckle of each finger, and the center of each finger covers the three tone holes on the front of the instrument. The home key for the left pinky is the E/B key.

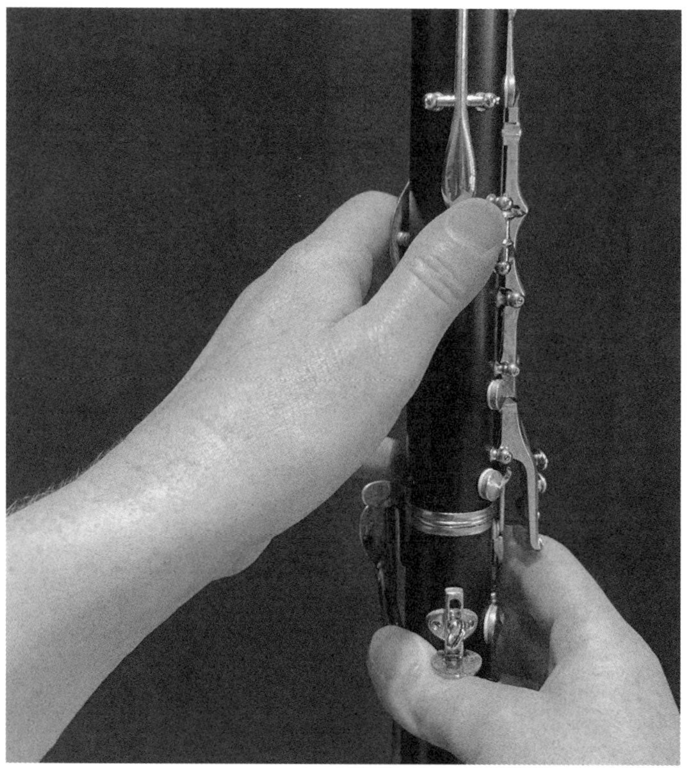

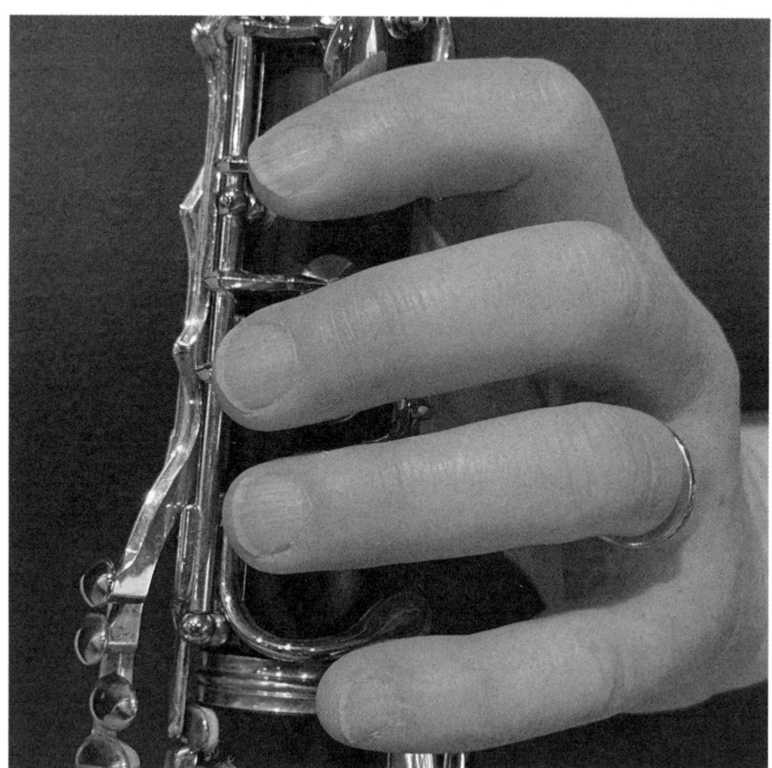

**TOOLBOX**

**Keep Your Head Up**

It's natural when first learning to want to look down at our clarinet as we play. However, having our head down will affect our air and create a bad tone. Instead, keep your head up, look forward, and bring the clarinet up to your mouth as you look straight ahead.

# Introduction to Reading Music

Music is organized on a staff of five horizontal lines. It is capable of displaying virtually all there is to know about a piece of music. Two important things it shows us is how music moves over space and time (rhythm) and how high or low the notes are (pitch).

Rhythm is organized horizontally along the staff. Pitch is organized vertically using the lines and spaces; the higher a note's placement, the higher the pitch.

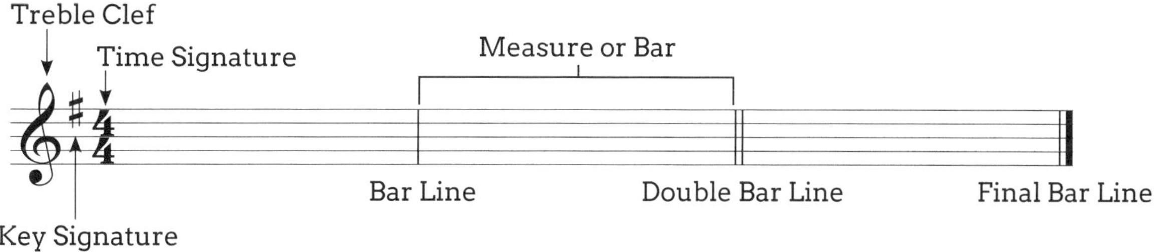


## Treble Clef

The treble clef establishes the second line as the note G. The symbol itself is an ornate G, also known as a G Clef. Notice that it curls around the second line to establish G. There are other clefs, but the clarinet only reads in treble clef.

## Bar Lines

Bar lines divide the staff into measures. A double bar line is used to mark something significant that occurs in the music, such as a new section. The final bar line is used to mark the end of the song.

## Measures

A measure is the space between bar lines. It is also known as a "bar." The movement of music (rhythm) is established from left to right through this space.

## Time Signature

The time signature determines how many beats are in each measure and what type of note receives one beat.

## Key Signature

The key signature assigns either sharps or flats (never both together) for particular notes for the duration of the song. This is covered in more detail in Lesson 3.

## Spaces

Notes in the spaces in ascending order happen to spell the word FACE.

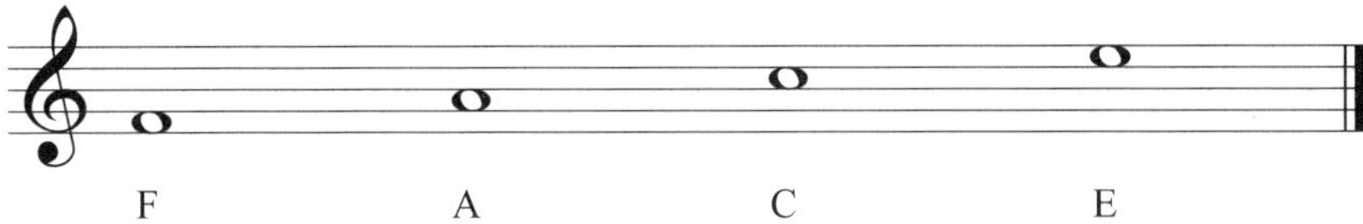


## Lines

An acronym commonly used to remember notes on the lines in ascending order is Every Good Boy Does Fine.

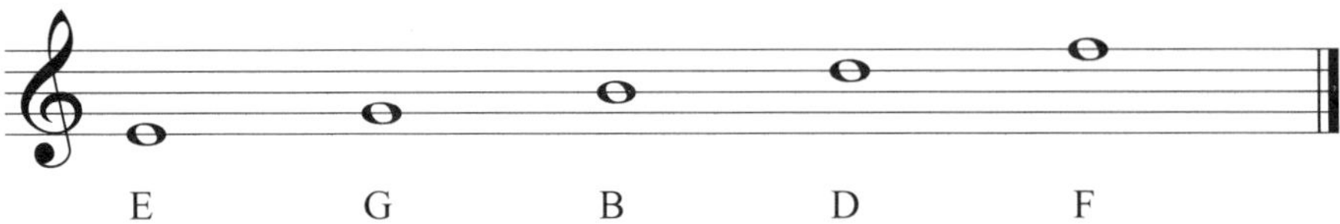


## Alphabet

When the spaces and lines are combined, you will see that music ascends alphabetically from A to G. You may find it helpful to memorize and locate A as you learn.

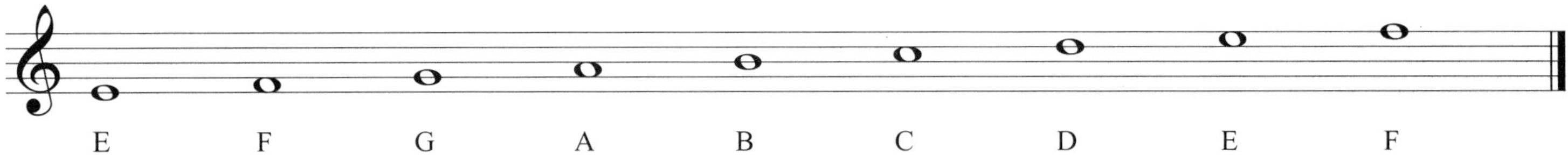


## Ledger Lines

The staff can be thought of as an infinite number of lines; five of them are visible and the rest are invisible. When a note is needed above or below the staff, small lengths of line become visible. For instance, high B is in the space above the first ledger line. Low C is on the first ledger line below the staff.

Notice that this is a continuation of the alphabet.

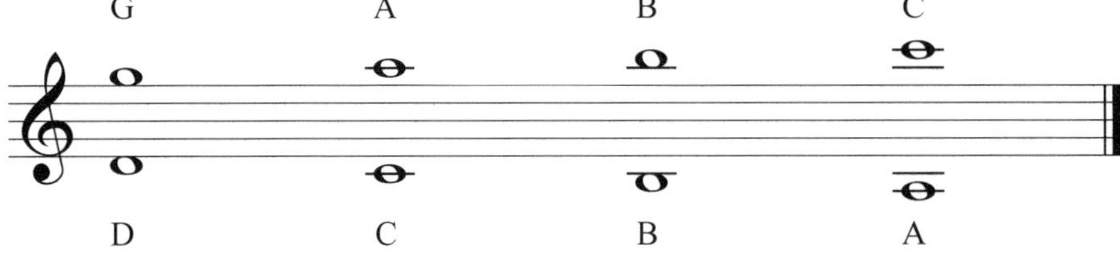

# Introduction to Counting Rhythms 

## Time Signatures

Rhythm is based on evenly spaced pulses that we call beats. The distribution of beats is determined by the time signature. The top number represents how many beats are in each measure, while the bottom number represents what kind of note receives one beat.

| | | | |
|---|---|---|---|
| 4/4 | There are 4 beats per measure<br>A quarter note ♩ is one beat | 6/8 | There are 6 beats per measure<br>An eighth note ♪ is one beat |

## Note and Rest Durations

The most common time signature is 4/4 time. The bottom number in 4/4 determines the following durations, whether sound (notes) or silence (rests):

**WHOLE NOTE & REST**
Each is four beats

**HALF NOTE & REST**
Each is two beats and
one half of a whole note

**QUARTER NOTE & REST**
Each is one beat and
one quarter of a whole note

**EIGHTH NOTE & REST**
Each is 1/2 beat and
one eighth of a whole note

**SIXTEENTH NOTE & REST**
Each is 1/4 beat and
one sixteenth of a whole note

## Beams

Eighth notes and sixteenth notes are joined by horizontal beams, typically in groups of two and four. Eighth notes can be joined together with sixteenth notes, as you will see in Lesson 6.

Throughout this book, you will find new musical rhythms presented with a clapping hands symbol. The video "Introduction to Counting Rhythms" will introduce you to a clapping and counting system that will help you learn these rhythms. Our time signature of 4/4 tells us that these first exercises have 4 four beats in a bar.

With your voice, count the four beats in each bar out loud. Clap the written notes, and do an *anti-clap* (open hands in time with the pulse) during rests. As our printed rhythms get more complex, this language of speaking rhythms will make it much easier for you to learn and automate new rhythms as your brain learns the patterns. Pause and practice individual bars or exercises repeatedly until it feels easy.

## Quartermaster

## Half the Fun

## Whole Lot of Fun

## Ar-resting

# Lesson 1:
# First Notes

## Embouchure

The way you shape your mouth on a wind instrument is called your *embouchure*. Place your top teeth on the mouthpiece about a quarter inch (1 cm) from the tip. Tuck the edge of your bottom lip over your bottom teeth, and then pull your lip and chin down. Bring the corners of your mouth in and around the mouthpiece so your lips are like a round rubber band.

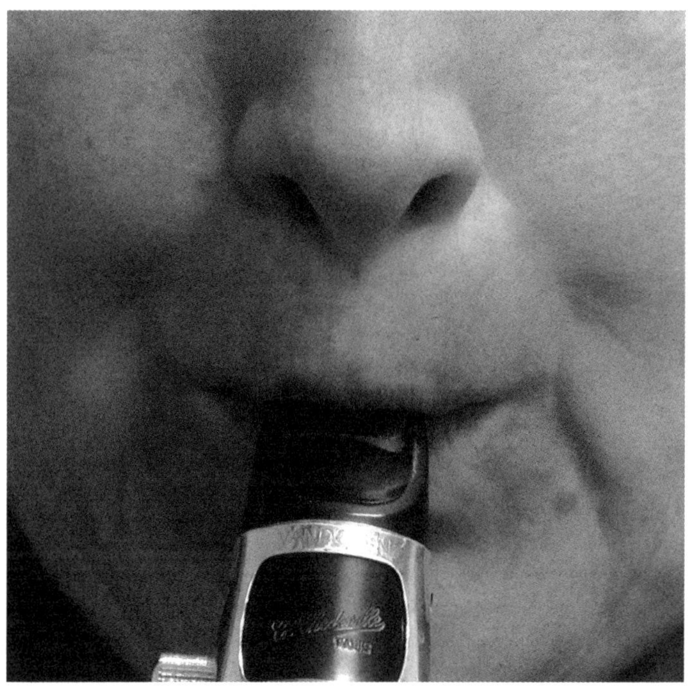

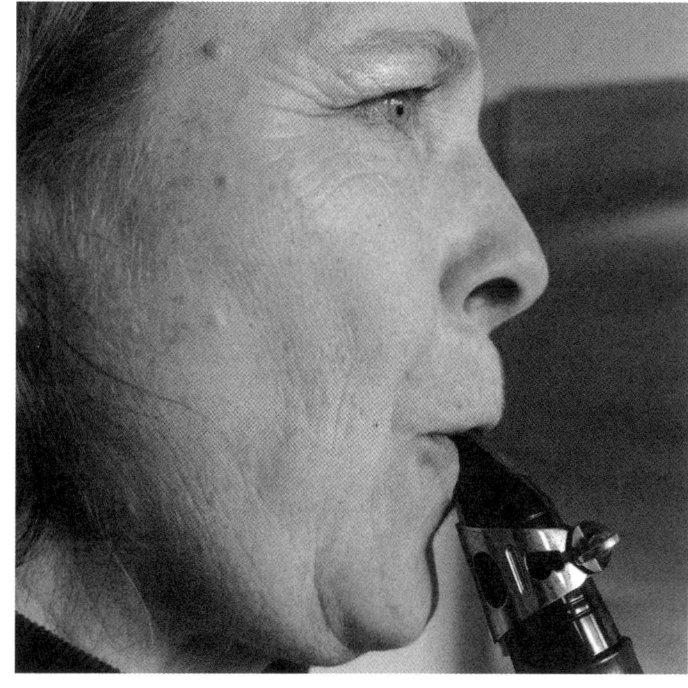

## Air

Blow fast, steady air to allow the reed to vibrate as much as possible. When you play any note, keep your air blowing steadily.

**CLARINET TALK**

**Squeaks**

Squeaks are a normal part of the learning process. Try the following things if you find a note squeaking:

1. Check how much mouthpiece is in your mouth. Too much mouthpiece will cause squeaks, and too little will cause a soft, weak sound.
2. Try not to bite down on the reed. Open your jaw (as if saying "ooh") to allow air to pass through and round the corners of your mouth to help release jaw tension.
3. Check if your fingers are covering the holes all the way or are accidentally pressing a key open. Looking in a mirror can help fix this.

## Introducing Your First Three Notes – E, D, and C

Our first three notes are on the staff lines and the fingering chart indicates which holes should be covered. For E, it is our thumb and index finger on the left hand. The D adds the middle finger, and C adds the ring finger to cover all three holes on the front of the top joint. Keep your fingers arched and relaxed. Watch the video for important tips for producing a good sound.

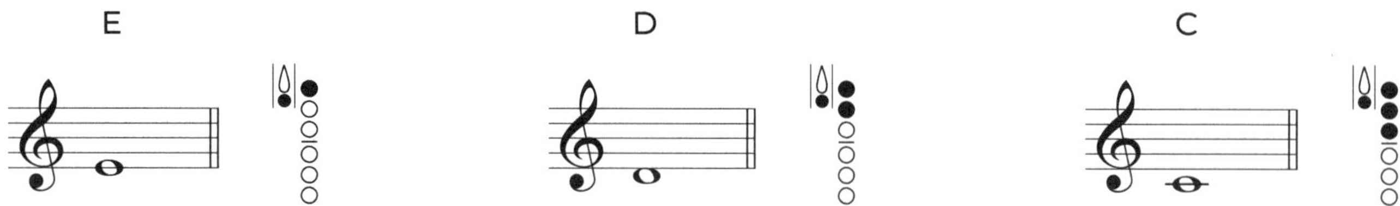


**NOTE:** You can access a PDF of all fingering diagrams and photos of each fingering online through the My Library page. Instructions on how to access this are on page 6.

Let's review your hand position before playing your first notes.

1. Your left thumb should completely cover the tone hole on the back of the clarinet. Angle your thumb up a little so the edge of your thumb is touching (but not pushing down) the register key.

2. Ensure your hand stays relaxed and your fingers are arched. Point your index finger up a little so it is touching (but not pressing down) the key above it.

3. Hover your fingers just above the holes. Keep your finger movement minimal as you move between notes.

4. Cover the hole completely. Watching your fingers in front of a mirror can help with this.

**CLARINET TALK**

**Using a Neck Strap or Thumb Rest Cushion**

If the clarinet feels heavy on your thumb, you can use a neck strap to help bear the weight. Neck straps will have a hook that attaches to a ring on your clarinet or a strap adaptor that connects to most thumb rests.

A thumb rest cushion is another accessory that can help make your thumb more comfortable. If you have mobility or pain issues in your right hand, there are also adjustable thumb rests that can be put on your clarinet by a professional technician.

These items can be purchased from your local music dealer.

## Whole Notes and Rests

A whole note is played for four beats and ends when the imaginary 5th beat (or beat one of the next bar) starts. Start your note on beat 1 and blow until the rest starts on beat 1 of the next bar.

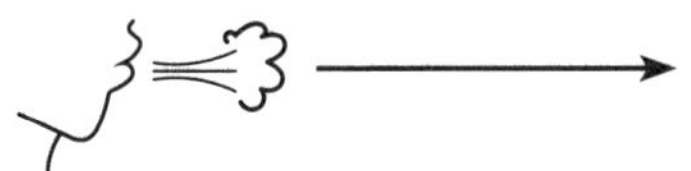

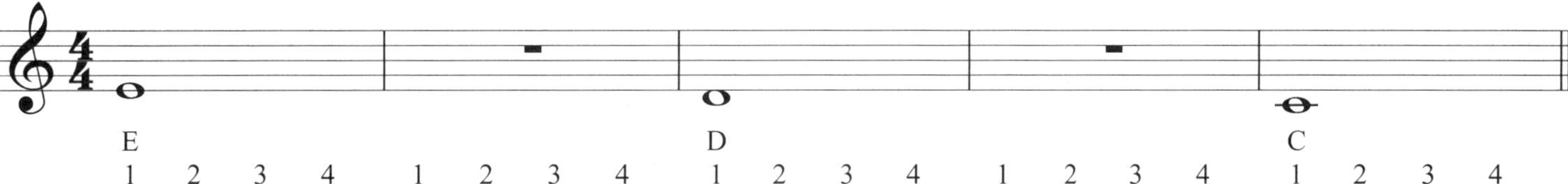


## Half Notes and Rests

This half note will end when the rest starts on beat 3.

## How to Articulate (Use the Tongue) on the Clarinet 

Clarinetists generally start notes with the tongue touching the reed, setting up a fast airstream in the mouth, and then releasing the tongue from the reed as if they are whispering "tee" or "tu." The tip of the tongue touches the top of the reed inside our mouth before we take our tongue off the reed.

Whispering these syllables on your reed and blowing very gently is a good way to practice tonguing. This helps set up the tip of the tongue to touch ONLY the tip of the reed.

## Steps for Tonguing:

1. Create a strong sound with your AIR ONLY on the first note, E.
2. As you blow the E with a beautiful sound, gently whisper "tee" or "tu," touching the tip of the reed with the tip of your tongue. It is best to use a quick, light stroke as your air is blowing. Be aware—it may feel strange or ticklish at first!

### Tee Time

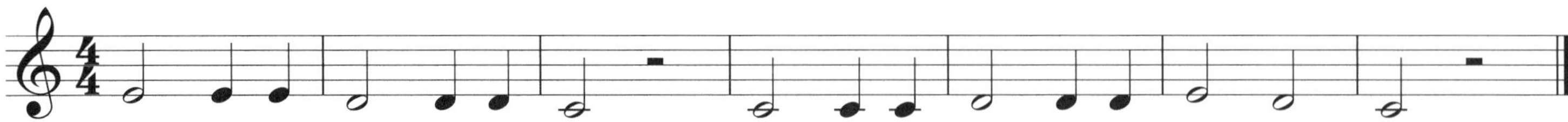


### Slurs

A *slur* is a curved line that connects two or more notes of *different* pitch. Tongue only the first note in a slur. When playing a slur, it is important to maintain steady airflow as you move your fingers to a different pitch.

### Tone Time

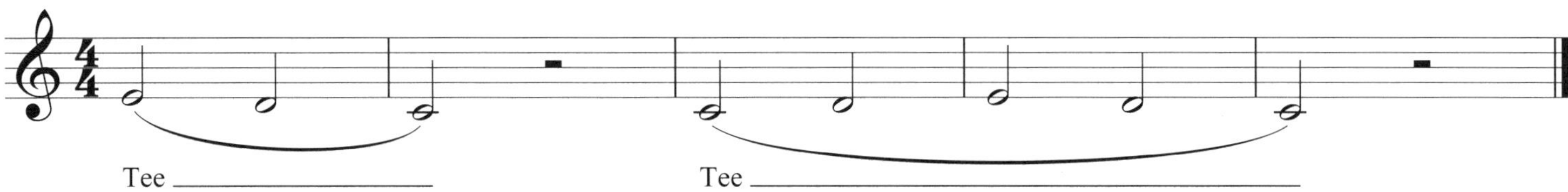


### More Tee Please

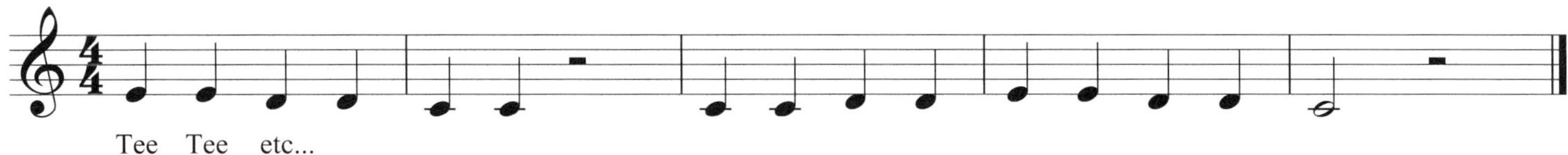


TOOLBOX

**Breath Marks and Phrases**

In music, a set of notes that make up a musical idea are grouped into a *phrase*. This is similar to how a group of words make a sentence. We breathe at the end of a phrase. Sometimes, a breath mark—which looks like a comma above the staff (,)—will suggest a good spot for you to take a breath. Other times, you choose to breathe where it makes sense musically. Rests are also natural breathing spots.

# HOT CROSS BUNS

Traditional

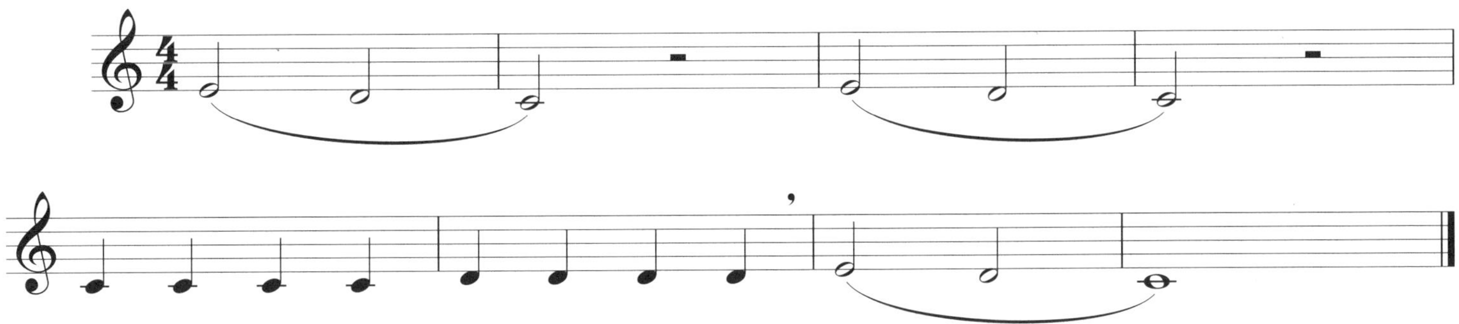



# MERRILY WE ROLL ALONG

Traditional

In the next example, try to play 4 bars in one breath. Take a deep breath before you start and again at the breath mark after bar 4.

# AU CLAIR DE LA LUNE

French Folksong

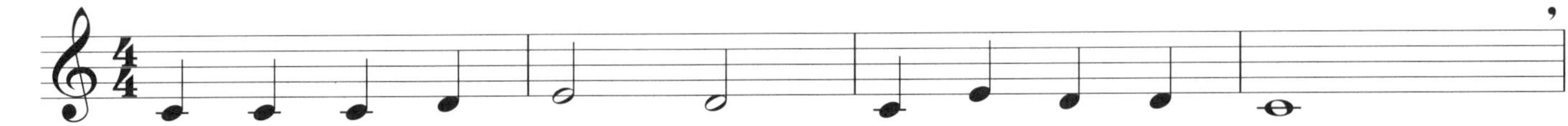

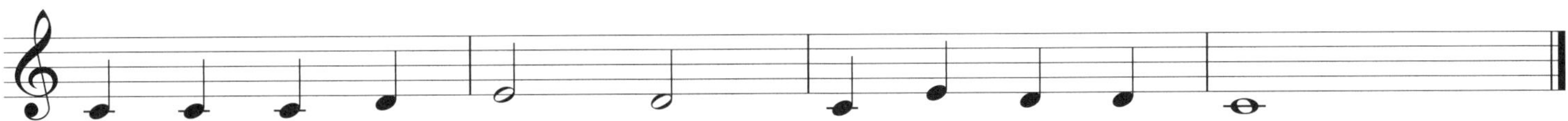

Each lesson has a duet for you to listen to and play along with. There is a demonstration track with both parts together, and a recording of each part separately. You can play with the same part as the audio track to match notes and style. Or you can play a duet by playing the top line on your clarinet while listening to the audio part of the bottom line and vice versa.

Each duet will have 'clicks' before the first note at the speed (tempo) of the music to help you prepare to play. "Three for Two" will have 8 clicks before the first note.

TOOLBOX

**Using a Metronome**

A metronome is a tool that provides an audible beat (such as a click sound) and a visible beat (such as a pulsing flash). They can be easily found as an app for your phone or other device. Practicing with a metronome is an excellent way to maintain rhythmic accuracy and develop a strong internal pulse. A metronome uses a measurement called beats-per-minute (BPM), often expressed as quarter notes per minute.

In the music below, a metronome marking is given at the beginning of the piece. This is a final tempo, so set your metronome slower when practicing. Once you can play the piece comfortably at the given tempo, try playing along with the audio. The clicks heard at the beginning of the audio are the same speed as the metronome marking in the music. You can also adjust the tempo of the audio on the MyLibrary page.

## DUET: THREE FOR TWO

# LESSON 2:
## Eighth Notes

Eighth notes are half the length of quarter notes. In 4/4 time, you can fit two eighth notes in one beat, so they each get half a beat. They look like quarter notes with a beam joining two or more together. Single eighth notes have a flag hanging from the stem. We speak the word "and" to subdivide the beat while counting.

### Introducing Eighth Notes

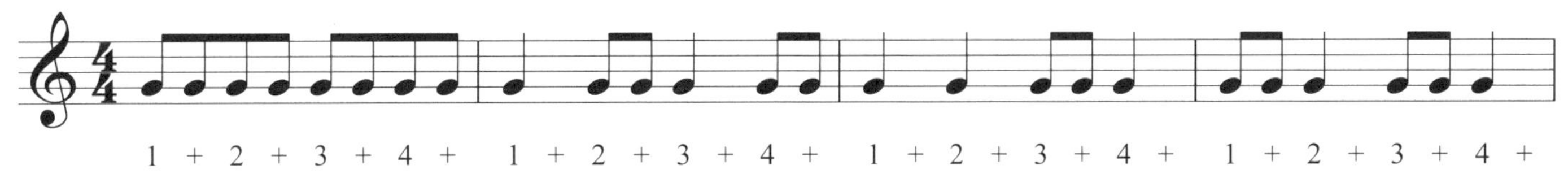

### New Notes

F

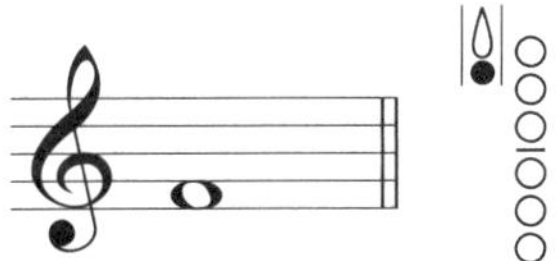

G

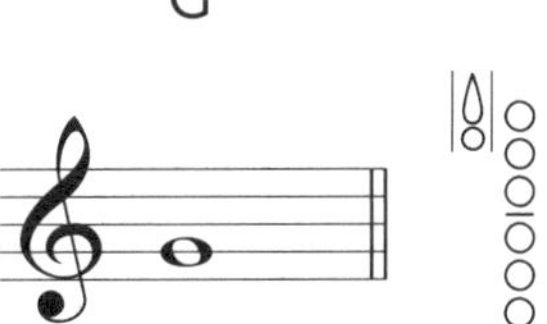

The G has no holes closed and is often called open G. Ensure that your fingers and thumb are always close to the holes and in a relaxed, arched position.

### Limber Left Hand

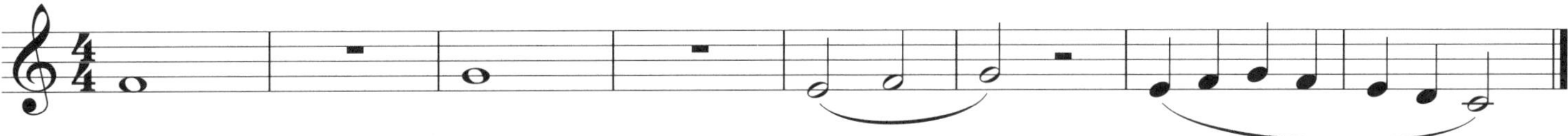

# WE WILL ROCK YOU

Words and Music by Brian May

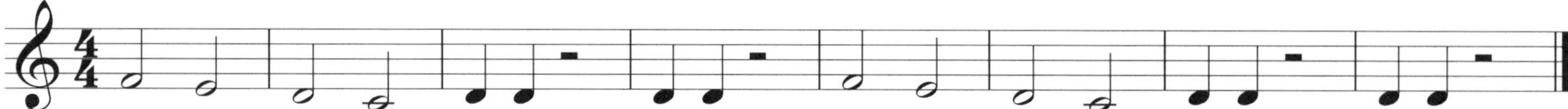



## Introducing Loopy Loops

When we train ourselves to play a musical instrument, our body develops a "muscle memory" that makes things feel automatic. Our goal is to develop this quickly so that we can learn music more easily. Throughout this book, you'll find "Loopy Loops," which are patterns that you should repeat five to ten times daily over the course of a week until the notes feel easy and automatic.

TOOLBOX

**Repeat Signs**

The two dots at the end of a double bar indicate that you repeat either back to the beginning of the piece or to the previous repeat sign.

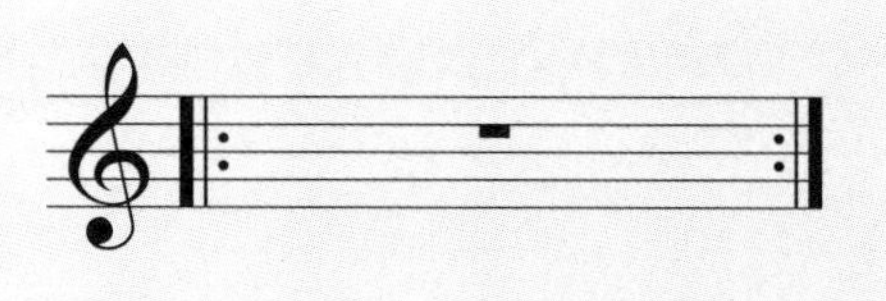

For Loopy Loops in this book, repeat each section five to ten times before moving to the next repeated section.

### Loopy Loops Left Hand

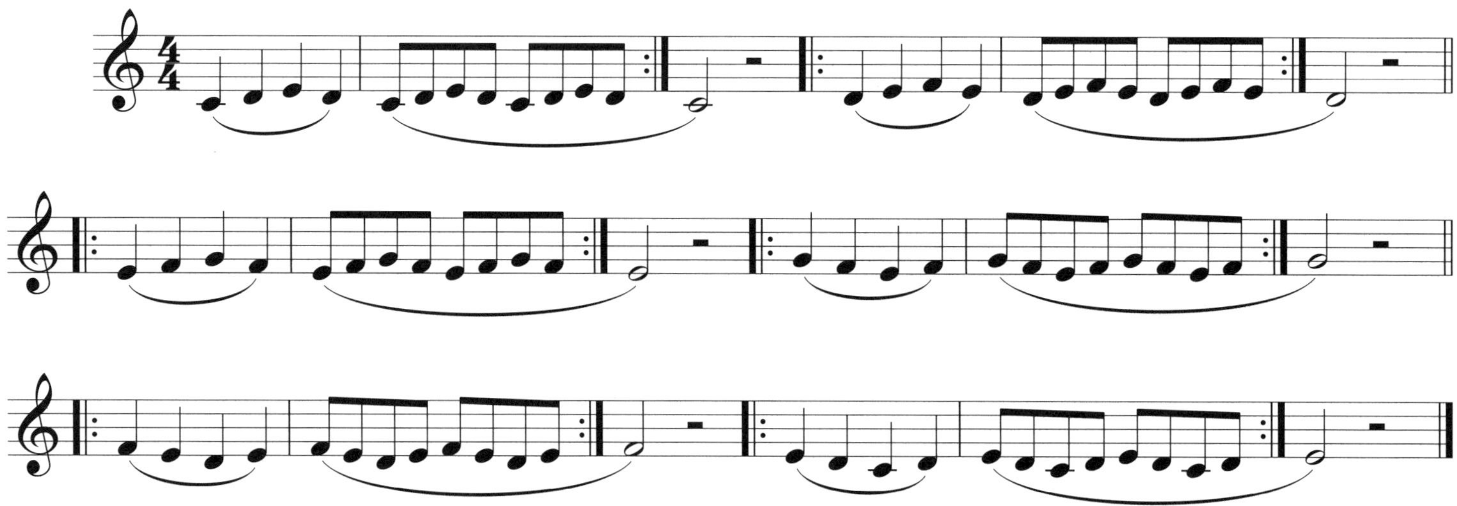

TOOLBOX

**1st and 2nd Endings**

Play through the 1st ending like a standard repeat sign and return to the beginning. On the second time through, skip the 1st ending and play the 2nd ending.

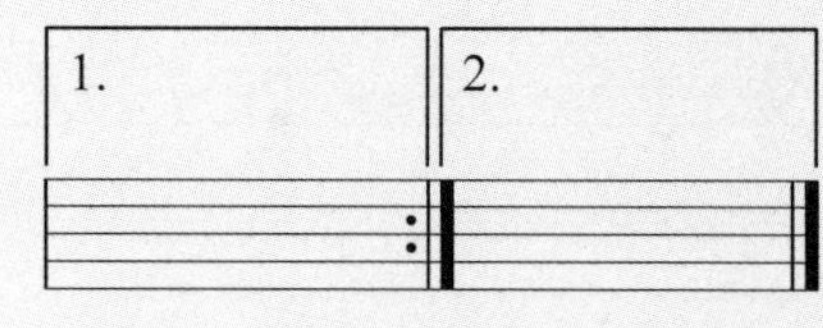

# MAMMA MIA

Words and Music by Benny Andersson, Bjorn Ulvaeus and Stig Anderson

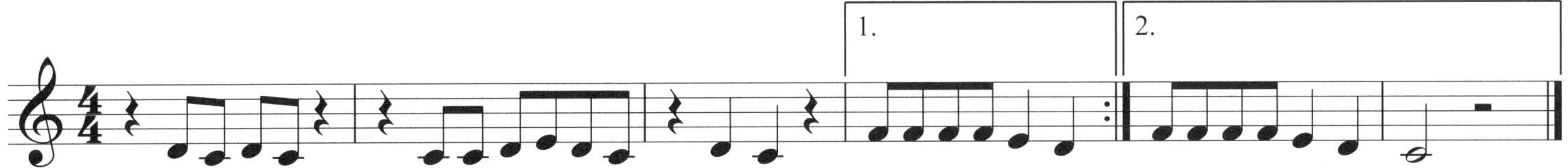




# EVERY BREATH YOU TAKE

Music and Lyrics by Sting

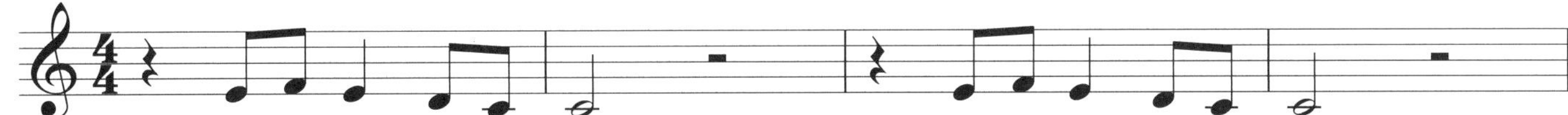

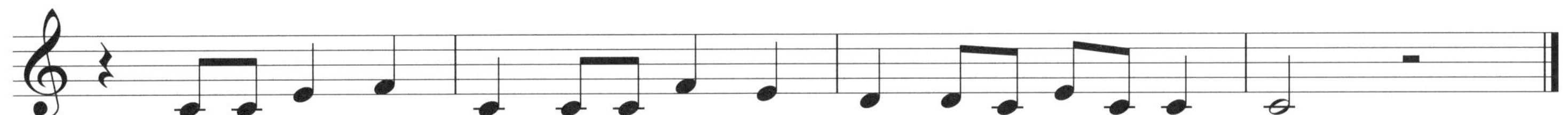



TOOLBOX

**Ties**

A *tie* is a curved line that joins two notes of the *same* pitch. Play one note for the combined counts of the tied notes. For example, a half note tied to a whole note is held for six beats. You will only tongue the first note in a tie.

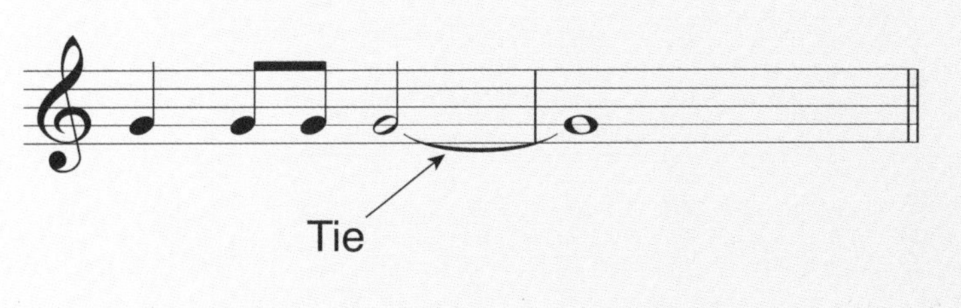


## Don't Tie Me Down

# BLACKBIRD

Words and Music by John Lennon and Paul McCartney

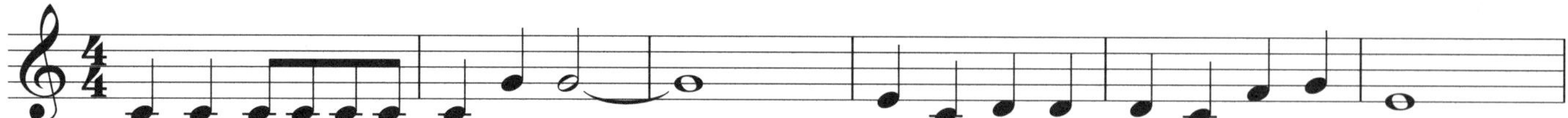

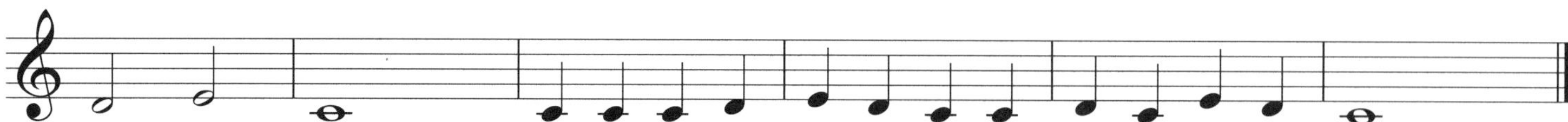



Notice that near the end of "Love Me Do," there is a tie and slur together. This note is held for five beats.

# LOVE ME DO

Words and Music by John Lennon and Paul McCartney

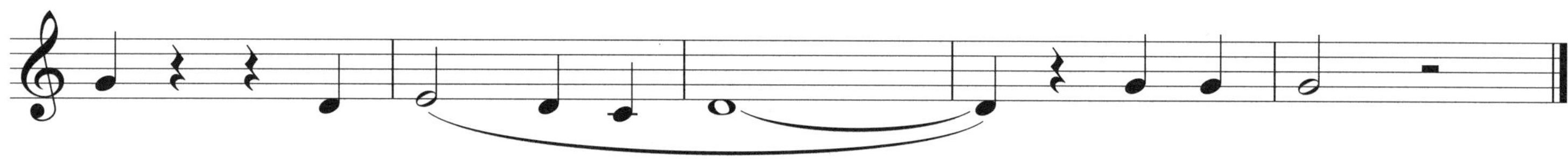



TOOLBOX

**3/4 Time**

Remember, a *time signature* tells us how many beats are in a bar and what type of note gets one beat.

**3** = Three beats in each measure
**4** = A quarter note receives one beat

## Three for a Bar

## THE CLARINET FROM THE ORCHESTRA SONG

Austrian Folk Song

## DUET: SIMPLE GIFTS

Traditional Shaker Hymn

# LESSON 3:
# Accidentals and Key Signatures

## Musical Steps

A *half step* (*semitone*) is the smallest interval (distance) between two notes. *Accidentals* alter a note by a half step in the following ways:

Accidentals remain for an entire bar unless another accidental appears before the end of the bar.

## New Note: F-Sharp

The sharp sign goes in front of a note on the musical staff, even though when speaking, we call it F-sharp. Remember when you lift your thumb to keep it close to the hole.

### Looking Sharp

Repeat this finger pattern until it feels easy and natural. Keep your fingers relaxed and close to the holes.

### The Keys to F Natural

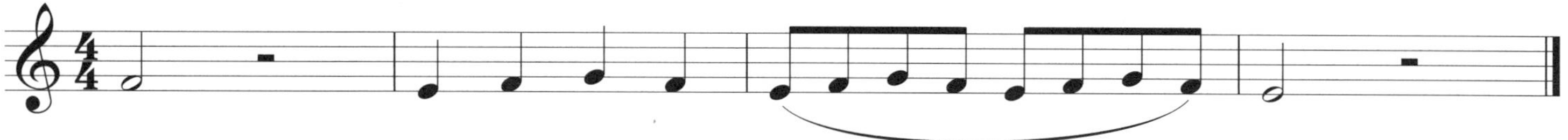

## Key Signature

Many songs are written in musical keys that have consistent sharp or flat notes throughout the piece. We use a *key signature* to indicate this. A key signature is located between the treble clef and the time signature. In the example below, both F's are sharp. Even though the sharp is placed on the top line of the staff, it applies to any F found within the music. A key signature with one sharp is called the "key of G." A key signature with no sharps of flats is called the "key of C."

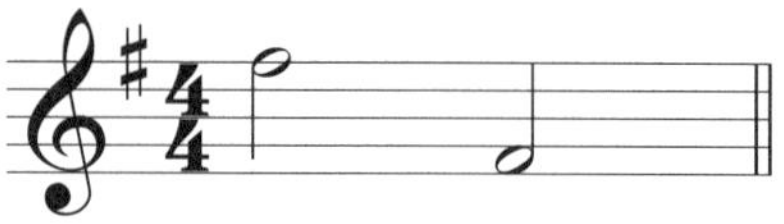

In the following example, notice the F-sharp in the key signature. All F's are sharp, so this will sound different from "The Keys to F" played previously.

### The Keys to F-Sharp

## SHARPER HOT CROSS BUNS

Traditional

## New Notes

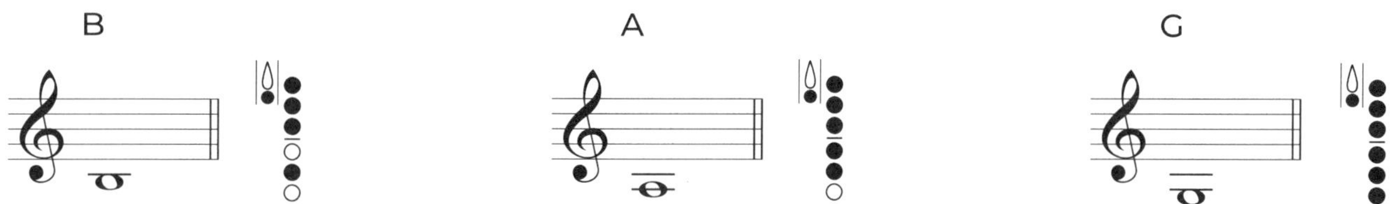


As you put the fingers of your right hand down for these new notes, keep them arched and relaxed. Your fingers should always hover close to the holes that they usually cover.

### Right Hand Ready

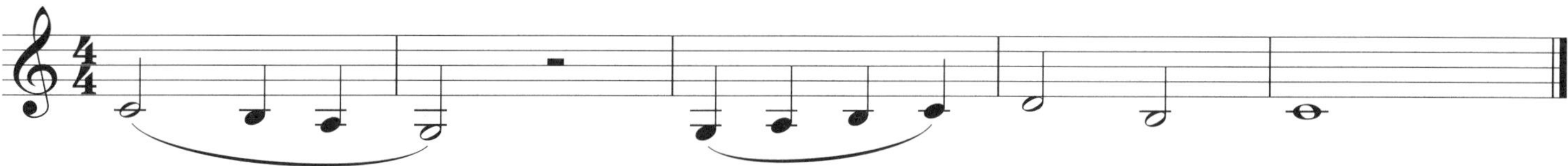

Repeat the following finger patterns until each one feels automatic. Look in a mirror to ensure that your fingers are covering the holes.

### Right Hand Loopy Loop

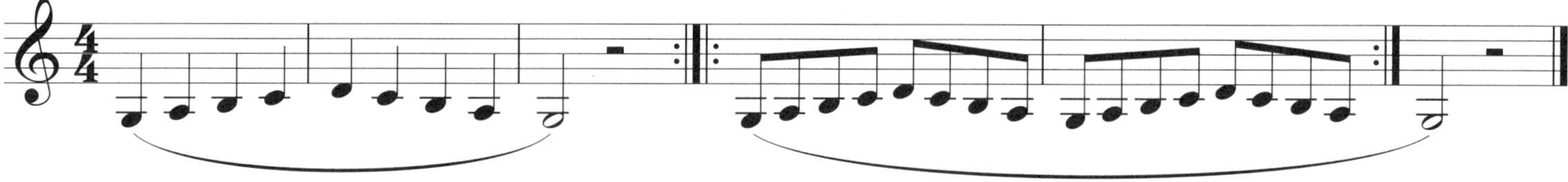

# FRÈRE JACQUES (ARE YOU SLEEPING?)

Traditional

# LOVE ME TENDER

Words and Music by Elvis Presley and Vera Matson

## Dotted Notes

A *dot* after a note adds half the time value to what the note is usually worth. A half note is two beats. If there is a dot after it, we add half of two or one extra beat for a total of three beats. A dotted quarter note is worth one and a half beats.

𝅗𝅥. = 𝅗𝅥 + ♩ = 3 beats
2 + 1 = 3

♩. = ♩ + ♪ = 1½ beats
1 + ½ = 1½

The tie in bar 2 makes the first note one and a half beats long. The dotted quarter note in bar 3 is also one and a half beats long, which makes those two bars identical in sound.

## Dotted Rhythm Trainer

> **TOOLBOX**
>
> **Pickup Notes**
> Sometimes, a piece of music has a lead-in note or notes. These are called *pickup notes*. They will appear as extra notes before the first bar. Music often has a bit of an emphasis on beat one, so the pickup note will feel like it is leading into this.

In "Spring," you will hear 7 clicks before the pickup note on the recording. If you are playing the top line, you will play on the "8th" beat. If you are playing the bottom line, you will start on beat 1.

# DUET: SPRING

### from the FOUR SEASONS

By Antonio Vivaldi

♩ = 112

# LESSON 4:
# Building Our Musical Vocabulary

## Tempo Markings

In music, we refer to the speed of the music as the *tempo*. Some musical terms give clues to the tempo, and many come from Italian words. Marked tempos are end goals; when first learning a melody, play it much slower than the marked tempo and gradually increase your speed as you feel comfortable.

| TEMPO | | |
|---|---|---|
| Italian | Definition | BPM (Beats per Minute) |
| Largo | Very slowly | ♩ = 40-60 |
| Adagio | Slowly | ♩ = 60-80 |
| Andante | Walking pace | ♩ = 80-108 |
| Moderato | Moderate | ♩ = 108-120 |
| Allegro | Fast | ♩ = 120-156 |
| Vivace | Very fast | ♩ = 156-176 |
| Presto | Very, very fast | ♩ = 176 and up |

## Dynamics

Indications of how soft or loud the music should be are called *dynamics*. They are usually abbreviated in one or two letters. Adding dynamics makes music more interesting and expressive. Dynamic markings are an example of Italian words that are standard in published music.

***p*** = piano or soft
***mp*** = mezzo-piano or medium-soft
***mf*** = mezzo-forte or medium-loud
***f*** = forte or loud

## ODE TO JOY

Music by Ludwig van Beethoven

## Crescendo and Decrescendo

*Crescendo (cresc.)* means to gradually get louder, and *decrescendo (decresc.)* means to gradually get softer. Arrow shapes (often nicknamed *hairpins*) indicate these dynamic effects.

**crescendo** **decrescendo**

# MY HEART WILL GO ON (LOVE THEME FROM 'TITANIC')

from the Paramount and Twentieth Century Fox Motion Picture TITANIC

Music by James Horner

Lyric by Will Jennings

## Staccato

*Staccato* is an articulation indicating that the notes should be played short, in a light and bouncy style. There should be a brief silence between each note.

# JINGLE BELLS

Words and Music by J. Pierpont

Allegro

mp

1.

2.

f

f

# BABY SHARK

Traditional Nursery Rhyme
Arranged by Pinkfong and KidzCastle

## Scales

Many songs in Western music are based on *scales*. The most common is the major scale, which is an eight-note pattern, as written in the G Major scale below. Every major scale starts on a different note and has a different key signature. It is very helpful as a clarinetist to be familiar with scale patterns. Using them as a warm-up until these patterns feel automatic is a great skill-builder. Additional scales and arpeggios are included as a downloadable PDF. See Online Resources on page 6 for more information.

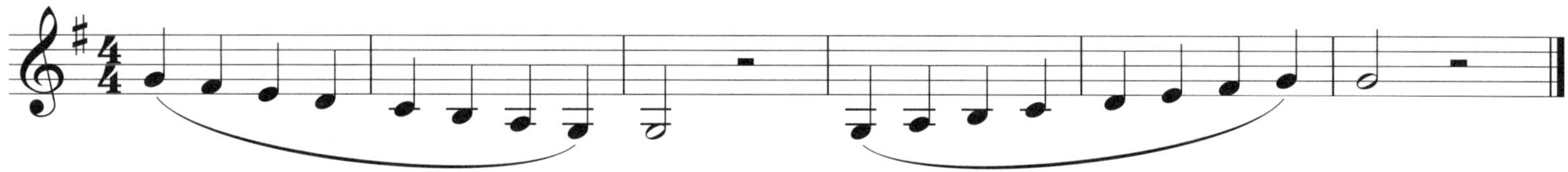

# JOY TO THE WORLD

Words by Isaac Watts
Music by George Frideric Handel
Adapted by Lowell Mason

# ARIRANG

Korean Folksong

## New Note: Low B-Flat

Remember, a *flat* lowers a note by a half step. When a flat appears as an accidental, it remains for the entire bar.

### Introducing B-Flat

In the next example, pay close attention to the key signature and accidentals—they change throughout! Accidentals in parentheses are called *courtesy accidentals* and serve as a reminder of what note to play.

### B-Flat or B-Natural

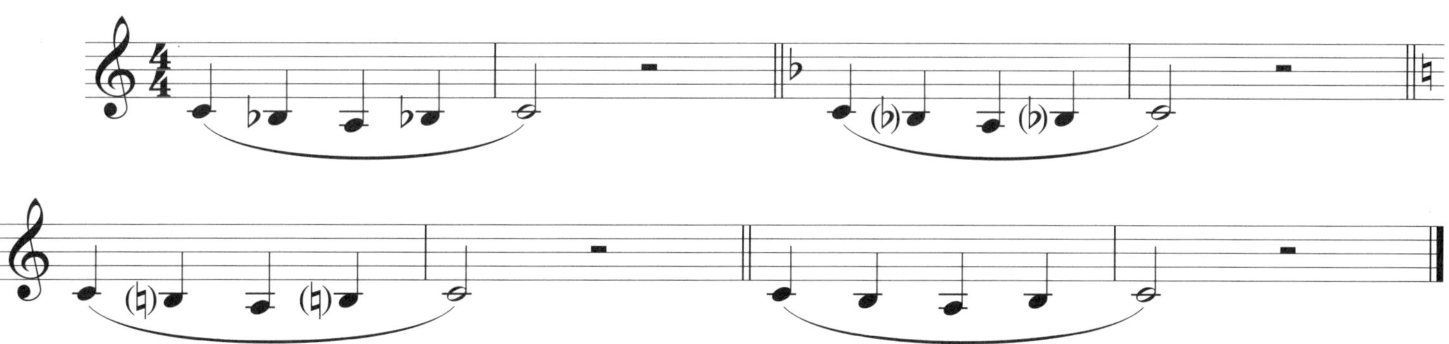

## New Note: Low E-Flat

Roll the side of your right index finger up to this E-flat key. The tip of this finder should remain hovering over the usual hole.

### Introducing E-Flat

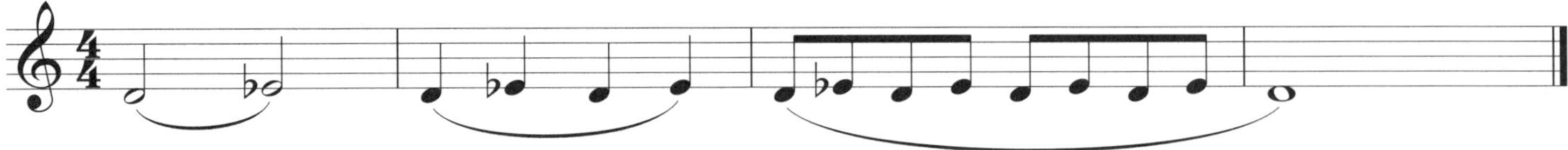

## LONDON BRIDGE

Traditional

## New Note: Low F Right and Left Fingerings

Some notes on the clarinet have more than one fingering. Use the fingering that is most natural for your hand; however, it is good to be comfortable using either one.

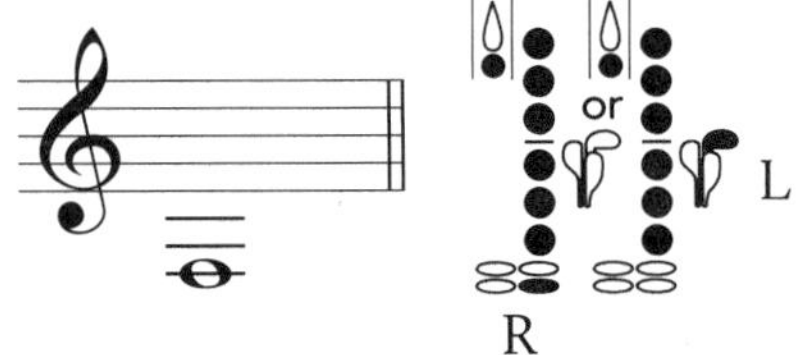


Try the exercise below using only the left pinky finger for low F, then repeat it using only the right pinky.

### Introducing Low F

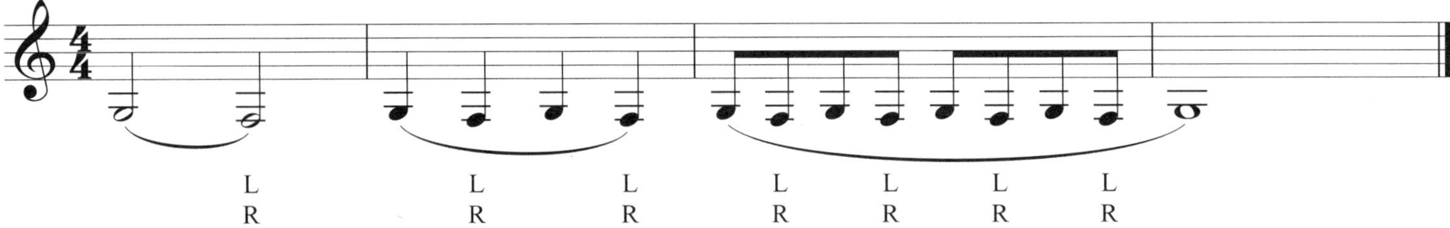

## Key of F

REMINDER: A key signature indicates whether to play a note sharp, flat, or natural. Flat (♭) or sharp (♯) signs are placed after the treble clef. The line or space that the sharp or flat occupies indicates which notes are changed.

This key signature has one flat: B-flat.

### All the Way Down to F

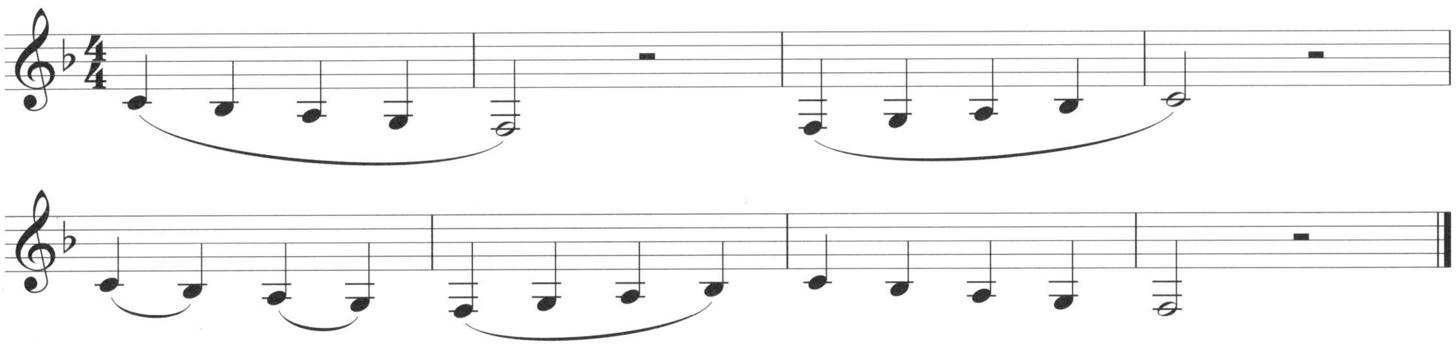

## Accents

The *accent* symbol (>) under or above a note indicates that we play it stronger. We can achieve this by using stronger air to emphasize the note.

### THE SLEIGH RIDE

Canadian Folk Song

## Eighth Rest

An *eighth rest* is worth half a beat.

### Eighth Rest Roundup

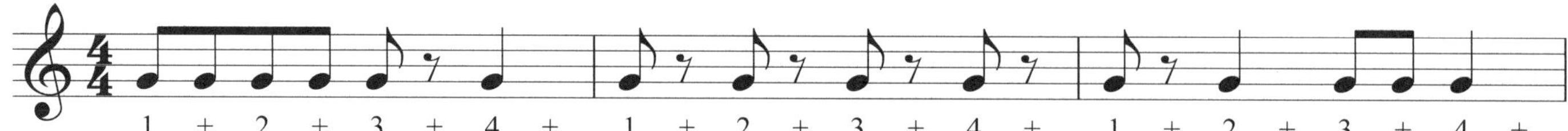

### Offbeat Eighth Notes

## Y.M.C.A.

Words and Music by Jacques Morali, Henri Belolo and Victor Willis

# BAD ROMANCE

Words and Music by Stefani Germanotta and Nadir Khayat

## Syncopation

Notes that start on the second half of a beat (or the "and" as we call it in our Rhythm Clapping Videos) are *syncopated*. Note that "Tequila" has a syncopated (or offbeat) pickup note to start the melody.

# TEQUILA

By Chuck Rio

## New Notes

*Covering the third hole on these notes will help to keep your left hand in a good playing position.

The A and B♭ require a mindful left-hand position for the best playing habits. Try fingering a low C and then add the A key with your top finger. This is a nonsense note, but it helps establish what part of your finger should hit the key. It is usually on the side of your knuckle, allowing your fingertip to hover over the hole it usually covers. When your left thumb plays B♭, use just the tip of your thumb, trying to keep your thumb hovering over the open hole.

Practice the next exercise in a mirror and see how little you can move your fingers and hands and left wrist.

## A-OK

# SHALLOW

## from A STAR IS BORN

Words and Music by Stefani Germanotta, Mark Ronson, Andrew Wyatt and Anthony Rossomando

Repeat each bar until it feels easy to do with light fingers that move as little as possible.

## Loopy Loop with B-Flat

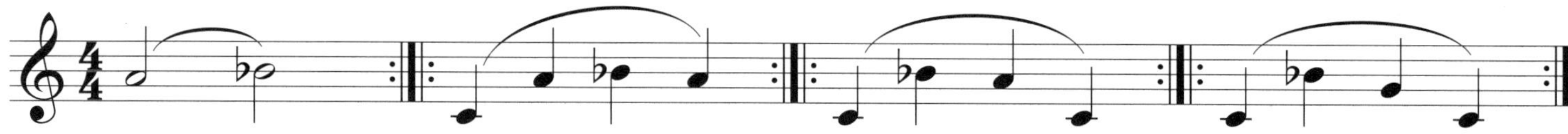

## Be Flat Out Loops

## Key of B-Flat

REMINDER: A key signature indicates whether to play a note sharp, flat, or natural. Flat (♭) or sharp (♯) signs are placed after the treble clef. The line or space that the sharp or flat occupies indicates which notes are changed.

This key signature has two flats: B-flat and E-flat.

# WHAT THE WORLD NEEDS NOW IS LOVE

Lyric by Hal David
Music by Burt Bacharach

**Slow Waltz**

# DUET: LEAN ON ME

Words and Music by Bill Withers

# LESSON 5:
# Chromatics and Enharmonics

## REVIEW

A half step is the smallest interval (distance) between two notes. A note is altered by one half step the following three ways:

**FLAT**
Lowers a note one half step

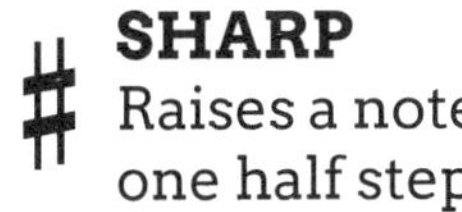
**SHARP**
Raises a note one half step

**NATURAL**
Cancels a sharp or flat

## CHROMATIC

*Chromatic* generally refers to notes outside of a given key signature, which are displayed using the above symbols. In music, chromatic passages move up or down in half steps (also known as *semitones*).

## ENHARMONIC

Pitch can be visualized as ascending from left to right, and descending from right to left. Every adjacent note is one half step apart. Two half steps is one *whole step*.

Every pitch has two names. For instance, the note between C and D is arrived at by either raising the C or lowering the D. The resulting C♯ and D♭ are *enharmonic* to each other; they are the same note.

There are two sets of notes that have nothing in between: E to F, and B to C. These notes are already one half step apart and contain enharmonic spellings as well, although you won't encounter them as often: E♯ and F, F♭ and E, B♯ and C, C♭ and B.

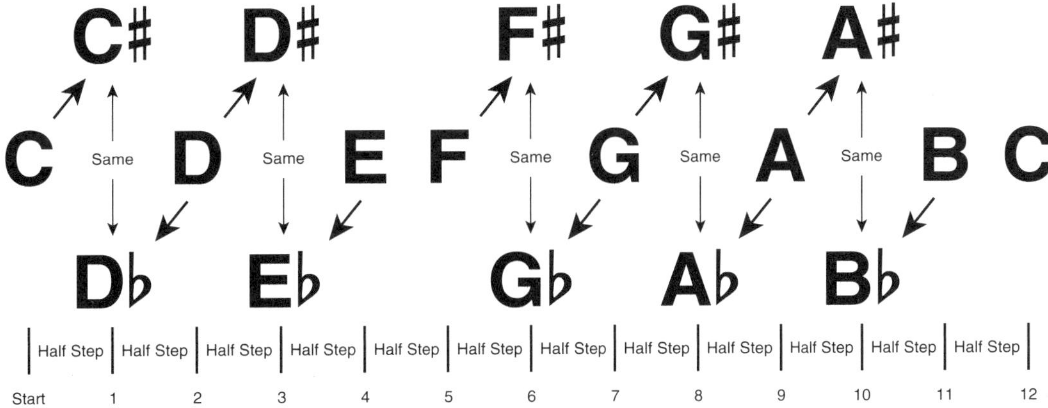


## QUIZ

Here are few questions to check your understanding:

1. What note is enharmonic to an A♭?
2. What note is one half step below E?
3. What note is one whole step above B (remember: a whole step is two half steps)?
4. What note is one half step above F♯?

**Answers:**
1. G♯ 2. E♭ or D♯ 3. C♯ or D♭ 4. G

## Chromatic Fingering for F-Sharp/G-Flat

To determine when to use chromatic fingering, look at the notes immediately before and after and choose the fingering that will create the smoothest transition.

When you have an F-sharp or G-flat beside an F-natural, use the chromatic fingering to produce a smoother transition. You should be comfortable with the fingering for both the regular and chromatic F-sharp. Music in this book is sometimes marked *chr* under a note as a reminder to use chromatic fingering.

In "Chromatic Capers," the notes in the first measure are F-natural, F-sharp, F-natural, F-sharp. Use the chromatic fingering for all F-sharps and G-flats.

### Chromatic Capers

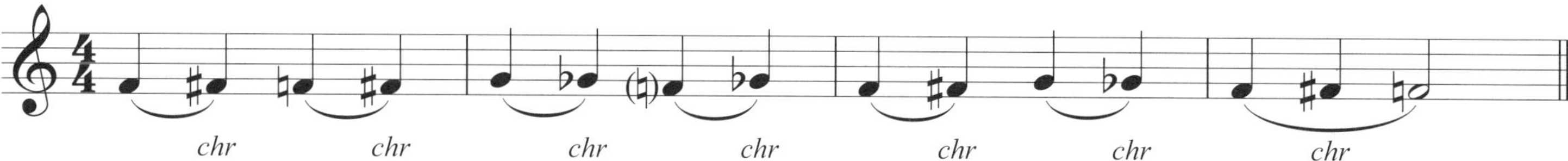


In the first bar of "Batman Theme," the third G is marked flat, so the fourth G in that bar will also be flat. The F on beat 4 is marked sharp, which will affect the last note of the bar. Use the chromatic fingering for all G-flats and F-sharps because they are beside an F-natural. Once an accidental is marked, it is valid for the entire measure, unless a new accidental appears.

## BATMAN THEME

Words and Music by Neal Hefti

In “Wipe Out,” use the chromatic fingering for all F-sharps.

## WIPE OUT

By The Surfaris

## New Note: C-Sharp/D-Flat

### Chromatic Capers Round Two

## DO-RE-MI

from THE SOUND OF MUSIC

Lyrics by Oscar Hammerstein II

Music by Richard Rodgers

## Key of D

This key signature has two sharps: F-sharp and C-sharp.

# PART OF YOUR WORLD

from THE LITTLE MERMAID

Music by Alan Menken
Lyrics by Howard Ashman

## Sharp-en Your Skills Loopy Loop

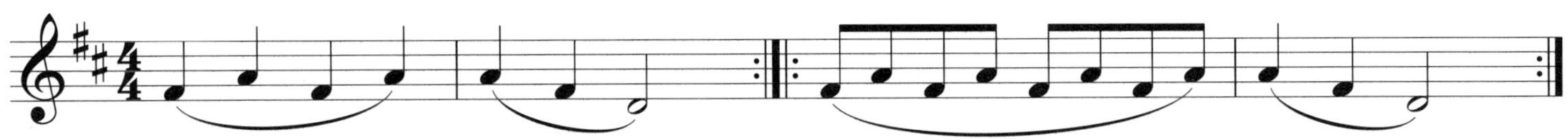

# MY DREIDEL

Traditional

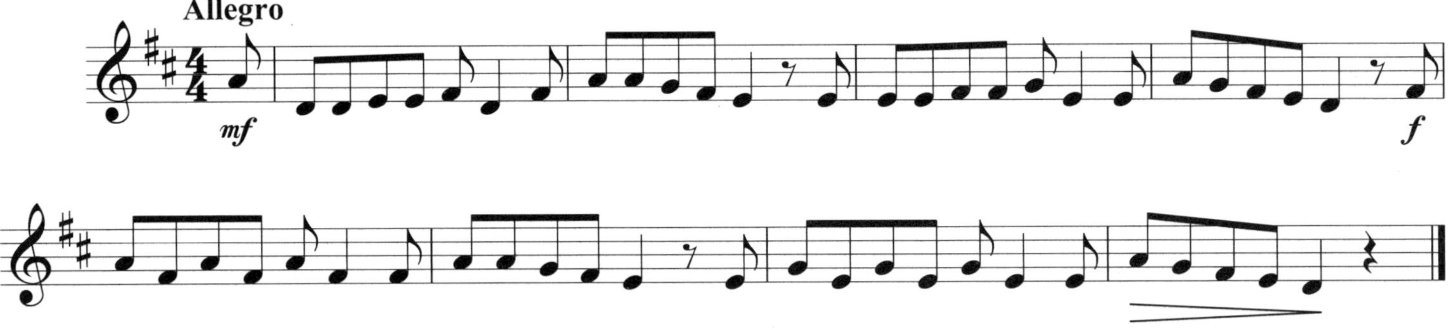

## New Note: Low F-Sharp

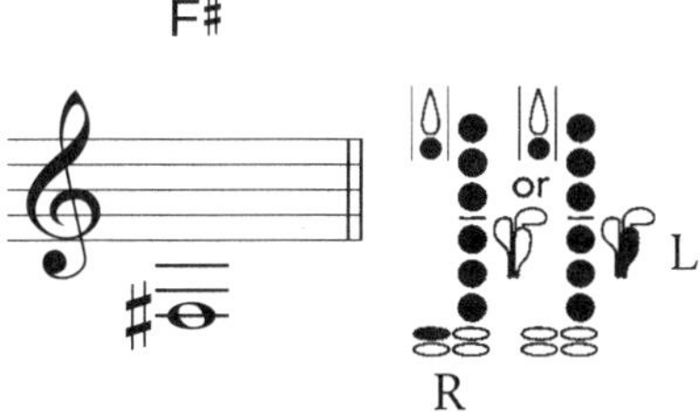


Try the "Sharpen Low F" exercise using only the left pinky for low F-sharp, then repeat it using only the right pinky. Use the one that is most natural for your hand; however, it is good to be comfortable using both.

### Sharpen Low F

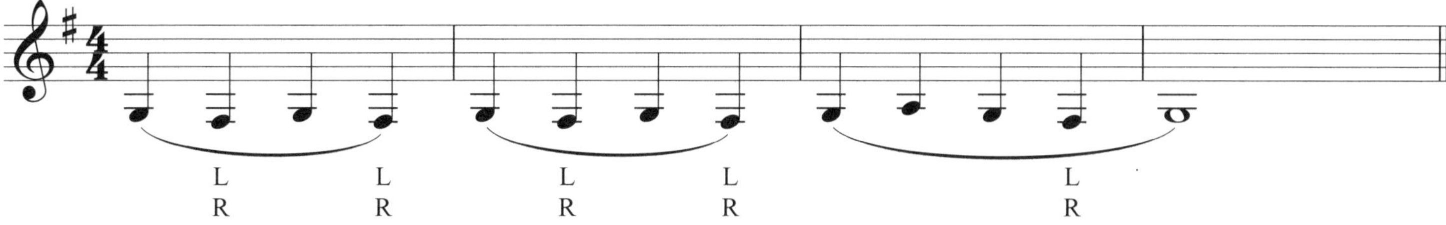


When you have two pinky notes side by side (like a low F-natural and a low F-sharp), you want to alternate sides, one on the left hand and one on the right.

### Put the Right Hand Forward (or the Left)

# MADE YOU LOOK

Words and Music by Meghan Trainor, Luis Federico Vindver and Sean Douglas

# DUET: OVER THE RAINBOW

from THE WIZARD OF OZ

Music by Harold Arlen

Lyric by E.Y. "Yip" Harburg

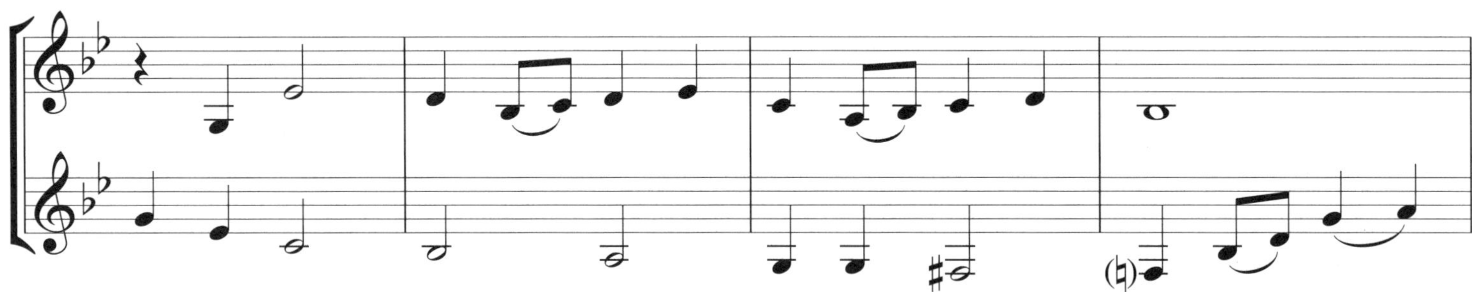

mf
mp
mf
mp
mf
mf
p
p

# LESSON 6:

## Sixteenth Notes

Sixteenth notes have two beams joining the notes together, and four fit into one beat in 4/4 time. You will hear in the video that we speak "one-ee-and-ah" in our counting language for this pattern.

### Introducing Sixteenth Notes

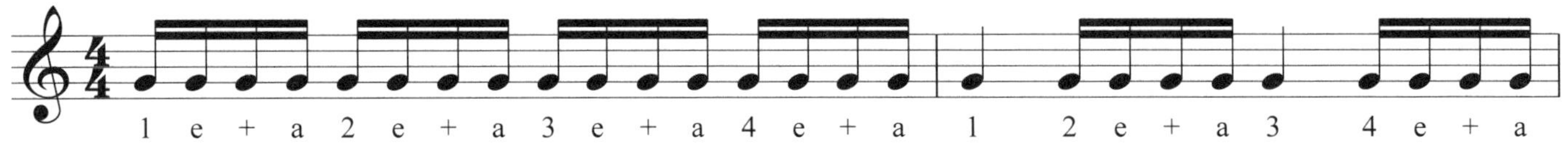


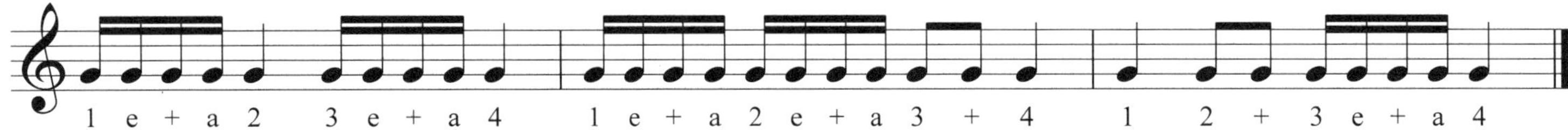


## THE GALWAY PIPER

Irish Folksong

### New Note: Low E

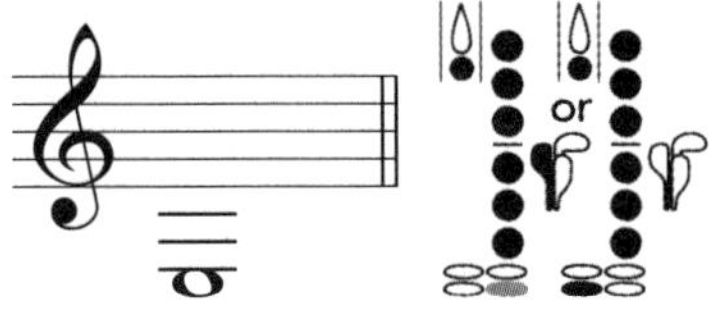


*Add the grey key if needed.

## Eek – Sad Mice

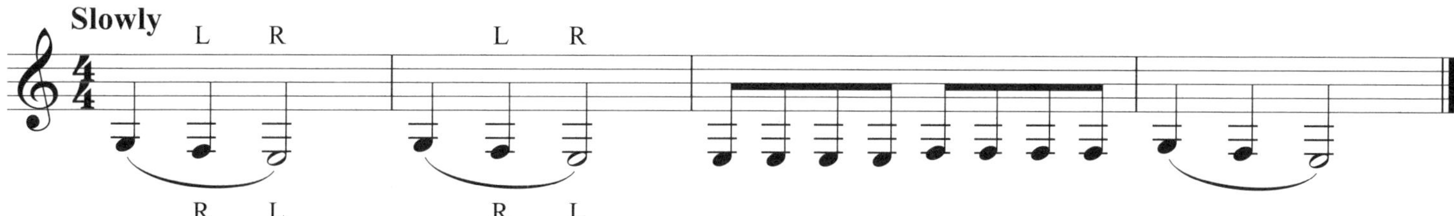


In "Theme from 'Jaws,'" try the E-F pattern first, with E on the left and F on the right. Then switch to E on the right and F on the left. Decide what is most comfortable for your hands, and that will be your usual fingering for these notes. It is good to be flexible with both.

# THEME FROM "JAWS"

from the Universal Picture JAWS

By John Williams

## New Note: Low G-Sharp/A-Flat

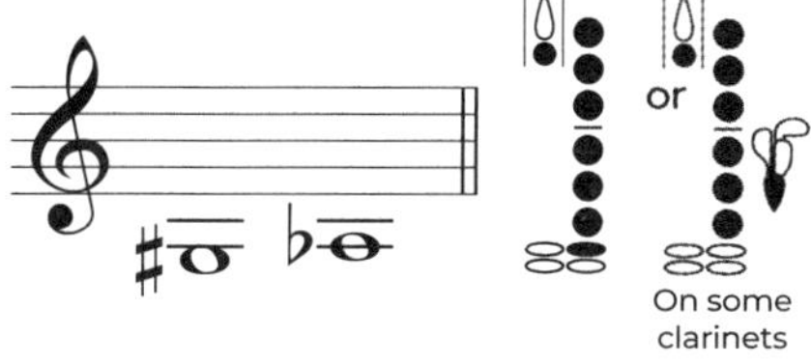


On many clarinets, there is no left-hand fingering for this note.

## Loopy Loop with G-Sharp/A-Flat

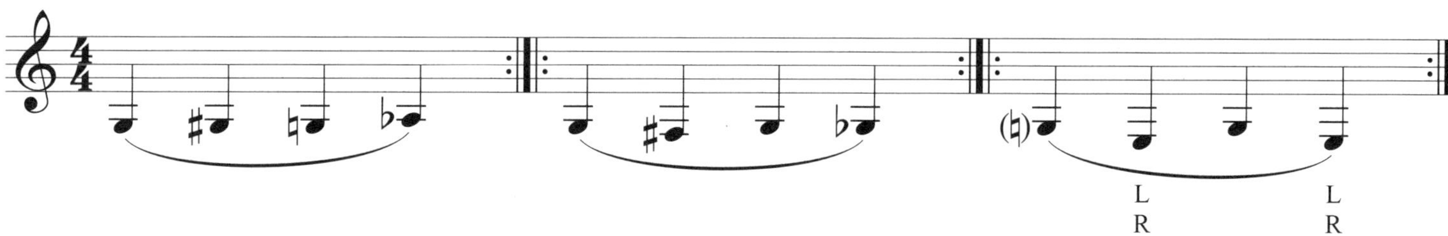

## Pinky Keys

Let's look at the pinky keys for your left and right hands. When you press a key with your left pinky, you can see that there is a corresponding movement on the right.

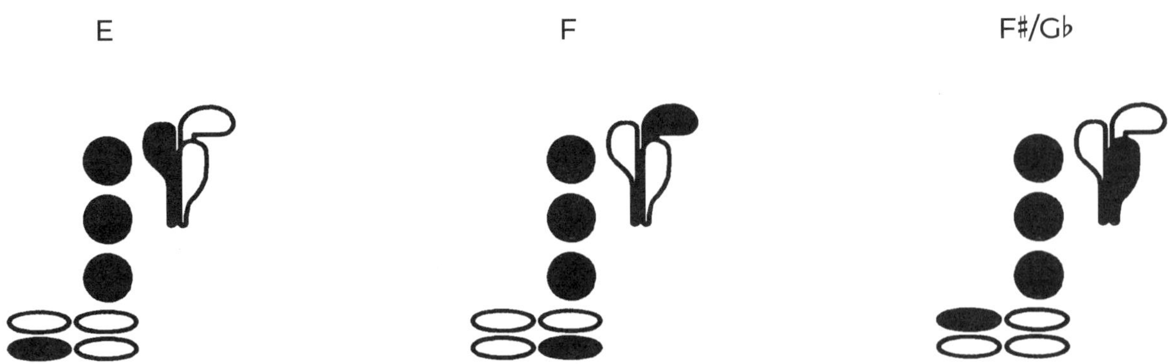


The only note that does not have a corresponding key on the left is the G-sharp/A-flat.

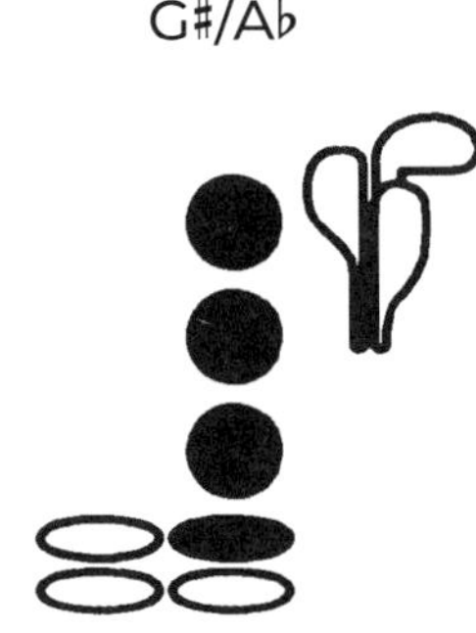


Start without playing and rest your clarinet on your right shoulder with the right hand. Use a mirror to watch your finger movement. Keep your hand, wrist, and arm relaxed as you move the pinky finger in circles counterclockwise and clockwise over the keys. When this feels easy and comfortable, try playing the right-hand notes, focusing on a full, strong air stream.

Repeat this process with the left hand, using your left shoulder to support the clarinet as you work on the pinky movement of the left hand. Use a mirror to ensure your fingers are completely covering the holes. A leaky hole will cause squeaks or will feel hard to blow.

## Pinkies Around the World

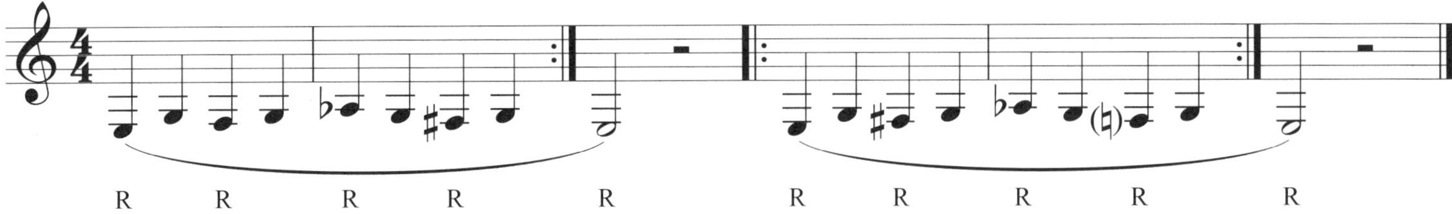


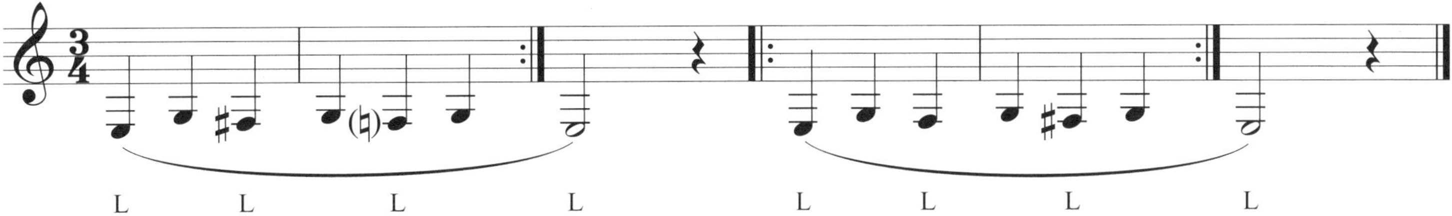


It is common to see eighth notes and sixteenth notes beamed together when they occur within the same beat. When an eighth note is beamed together with two sixteenth notes, it is counted as "1e-&-a, 2e-&-a, 3e-&-a, 4e-&-a," etc.

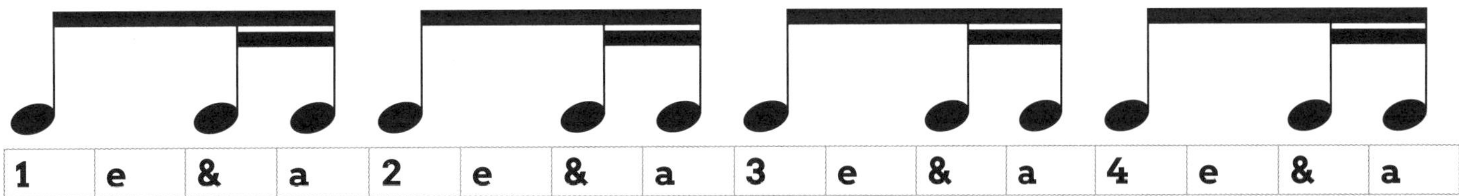


A dotted eighth note gets three-quarters of a count, and a sixteenth note gets one-quarter of a count. Together, they equal one full count. We generally count this as "1e&-a, 2e&-a, 3e&-a, 4e&-a," etc.

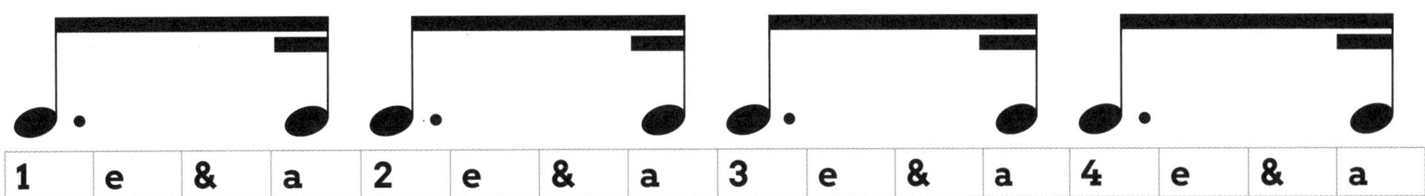

## Introducing Dotted Eighth and Sixteenth Notes

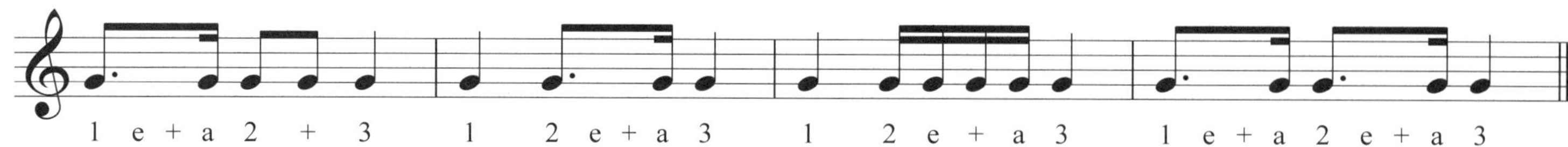


# ROW, ROW, ROW YOUR BOAT

Traditional

Pay close attention to the articulations and dynamics in "Alouette." Practice all elements slowly until you feel comfortable, then increase the tempo.

# ALOUETTE

Traditional

"Rhythmic Challenge" has several new rhythms. When learning a new rhythm, isolate the beat(s) it falls on and repeat just that section. Be sure to watch the video to learn how to count each one.

## Rhythmic Challenge

# HEY JUDE

Words and Music by John Lennon and Paul McCartney

**TOOLBOX**

**Swing Eighths**
Swing eighths is a type of rhythmic feel. In a pair of eighth notes, the first note will last a little bit longer than the second. So, in a set of four eighth notes, it will sound "long-short-long-short." This concept is best learned by listening.

# HAPPY BIRTHDAY TO YOU

Words and Music by Mildred J. Hill and Patty S. Hill

Blues in C

# DEEP RIVER BLUES

Traditional
Arranged and Adapted by Doc Watson

TOOLBOX

**Trill**

A *trill* is a musical ornamentation shown in music with a *tr* and sometimes a squiggly line for the duration of the note. You play a trill by playing the written note and then moving back and forth quickly between the written note and the note above. On long notes, you will move between the two notes many times. On shorter notes, it may only be once or twice.

# DAWN

from the William Tell Overture

By Gioachino Rossini

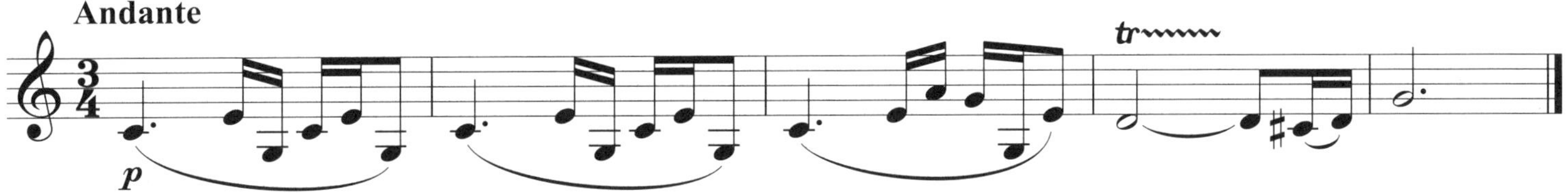




## Key of E-Flat

This key signature has three flats: B-flat, E-flat, and A-flat.

## New Note: G-Sharp/A-Flat

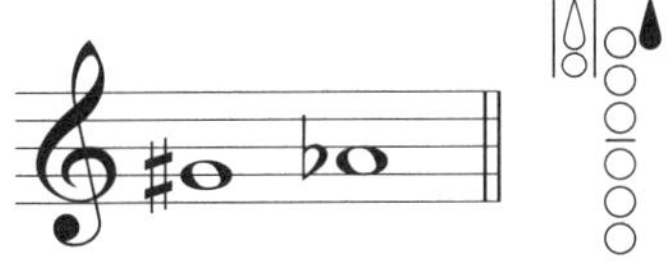

# EASY ON ME

Words and Music by Adele Adkins and Greg Kurstin

TOOLBOX

**Marcato**

This type of accent indicates that we play the note stronger as well as slightly shorter than usual. The initial attack of a marcato is the same as an accent, but you will also leave space after each note.

In "All You Need Is Love," you will hear 7 clicks before the pickup notes on the recording.

# DUET: ALL YOU NEED IS LOVE

Words and Music by John Lennon and Paul McCartney

f
mf
1.
2.

# LESSON 7:
# Triplets

## Eighth-Note Triplets

A group of three eighth notes with a 3 above it is a *triplet*. One triplet group fits into one beat. They can be counted as "1-trip-let, 2-trip-let, 3-trip-let, 4-trip-let." You can use other 3-syllable words like "blue-ber-ry" to count the rhythm.

Once you have a feel for triplets, practice clapping and counting aloud, switching between two eighth notes in a beat and triplets.

### Introducing Triplets

## ADDAMS FAMILY THEME

Theme from the TV Show and Movie

Music and Lyrics by Vic Mizzy

**TOOLBOX**

**Tenuto**

A *tenuto* sounds smooth and connected, with no break of sound between notes. It is marked as a line above or below a notehead. Stretch the notes to their full value so they are slightly emphasized with no space after the note.

# HABANERA

from CARMEN

By Georges Bizet

# A HARD DAY'S NIGHT

Words and Music by John Lennon and Paul McCartney

## New Note: Chromatic B

This alternate fingering for low B is the chromatic fingering. Use this primarily when you have a B-natural beside a B-flat.

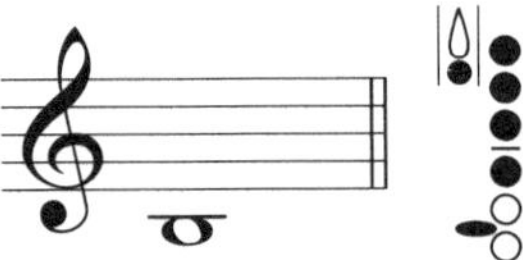

### Chromatic Fingering Drills

In the next examples, try each measure alone until you are accustomed to the fingering. Then, try them slowly as a complete song for extra finger practice. Review Lesson 5 and the Fingering Chart at the back of the book if you are unsure about any enharmonic note spellings.

### Chromatic Loopy Loops Upper Joint

Chromatic Loopy Loops Bottom Joint

# SUPERCALIFRAGILISTICEXPIALIDOCIOUS

from MARY POPPINS

Words and Music by Richard M. Sherman and Robert B. Sherman

# JAMES BOND THEME

By Monty Norman

## Triplets and Swing

Another way to think about swing eighths is that the two eighth notes are played as the first and third notes of an eighth-note triplet set.

In "Pink Panther," you will hear 7 clicks before the pickup note on the recording.

# DUET: PINK PANTHER

from THE PINK PANTHER

By Henry Mancini

f
f
mf
mp
mf
mp

# LESSON 8:
## Putting It All Together

Remember, focused practice helps you improve more quickly. Here are some tips to aid in your practice sessions:

1. Begin your practice session with exercises that focus on one aspect of your playing at a time. These include breathing and blowing exercises, finger patterns like Loopy Loops, and rhythm patterns like the clapping exercises. By focusing intensely on concepts of tone, finger movement, rhythm, and articulation for a short time each day, we create good habits that feel almost automatic.
2. Isolate a small section (two notes or a bar) and determine what feels challenging. If it's rhythm, clap it until it feels easy. If it's notes, play it correctly three times before adding back the entire phrase. If it's articulation, try speaking the pattern until it feels easy, and then play it on your clarinet.
3. Record yourself regularly. Most smartphones do a decent recording if you place it about 6 ft/2m away. Record a short section of your music, and then try fixing one thing. Then, re-record it. If need be, fix "the next thing." This should give you a good recording in one practice session. If you have time and energy, record the next section the same way. Even though it is not fun (at first) to listen to our recordings, this can help us improve much faster.
4. Do a video recording from time to time. Look for good habits in your playing. Are the corners of your embouchure coming in toward the mouthpiece? (Avoid smiling when you play; save it for afterward!) Is your breathing deep and relaxed? (Avoid shallow, gasping breaths.) Is your head looking straight ahead? (Avoid tilting your chin down.) Are your fingers arched, relaxed, and staying close to the holes? (Avoid flying fingers that slap the instrument.) Do you look relaxed? (Avoid tense shoulders, jaw, and hands.)
5. Play music that you enjoy, and be patient. You can improve a great deal in just a few months of regular, thoughtful, focused practice.

## Key of A

This key signature has three sharps: F-sharp, C-sharp, and G-sharp.

CLARINET TALK

**Fingering Tip**

On most clarinets, you can only play low G♯ with the right pinky. This means that any other pinky notes adjacent to the G♯ must be played with the left hand.

# STAR WARS (MAIN THEME)

from STAR WARS: A NEW HOPE

Music by John Williams

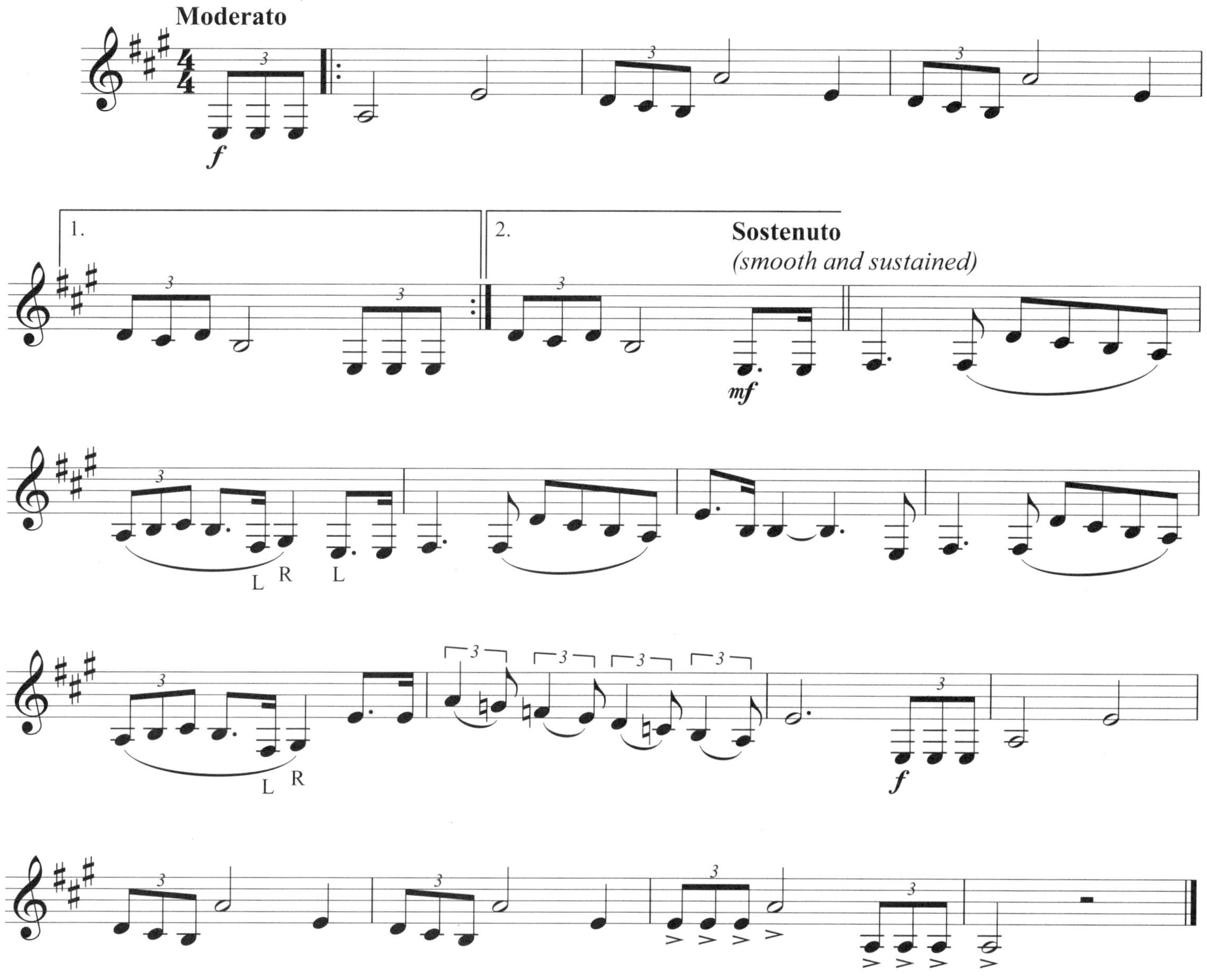
Moderato
f
1.
2.
Sostenuto
(smooth and sustained)
mf
L R L
L R
f



# TIDEO

Ohio Play Party Song

Moderato
f

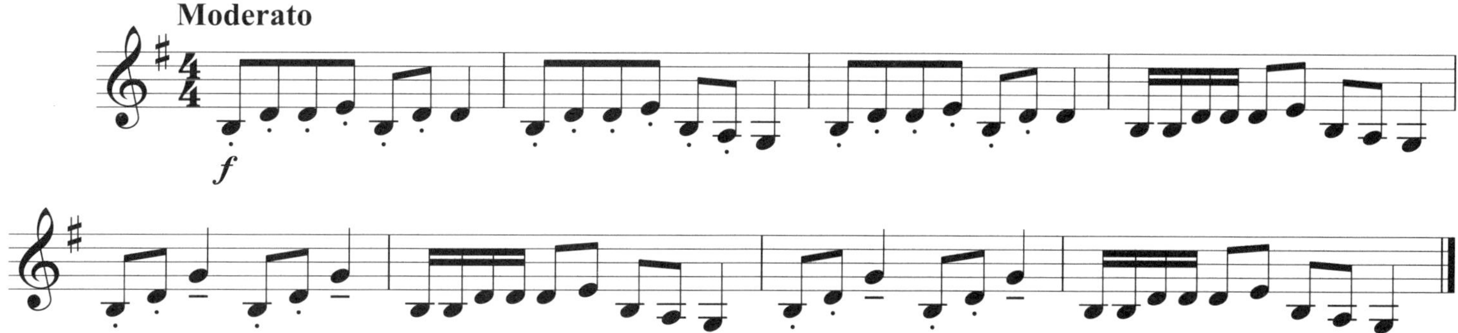

## Articulation Styles

***Staccato*** ***Tenuto*** ***Accent*** ***Marcato***

***Staccato*** – Make the note short (about half of the usual length), leaving space between notes.
***Tenuto*** – Make the note extra-long and connected. Sometimes, we lean on it gently with our air to emphasize it.
***Accent*** – Start the note with and more air than usual to emphasize it.
***Marcato*** – Short and accented.

Watch the video for a review of how to play the articulations we've learned thus far.

### Tongue Twister

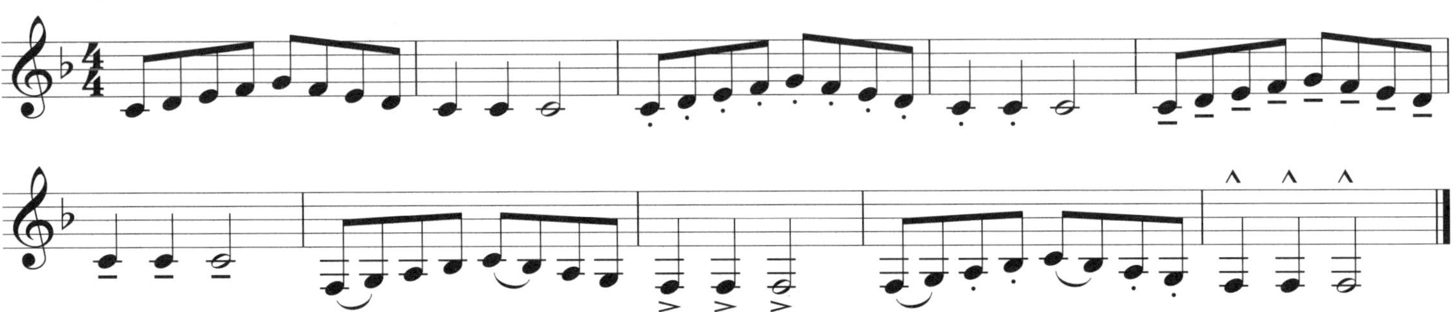

# KLEZMER CONTRA

Folk Song

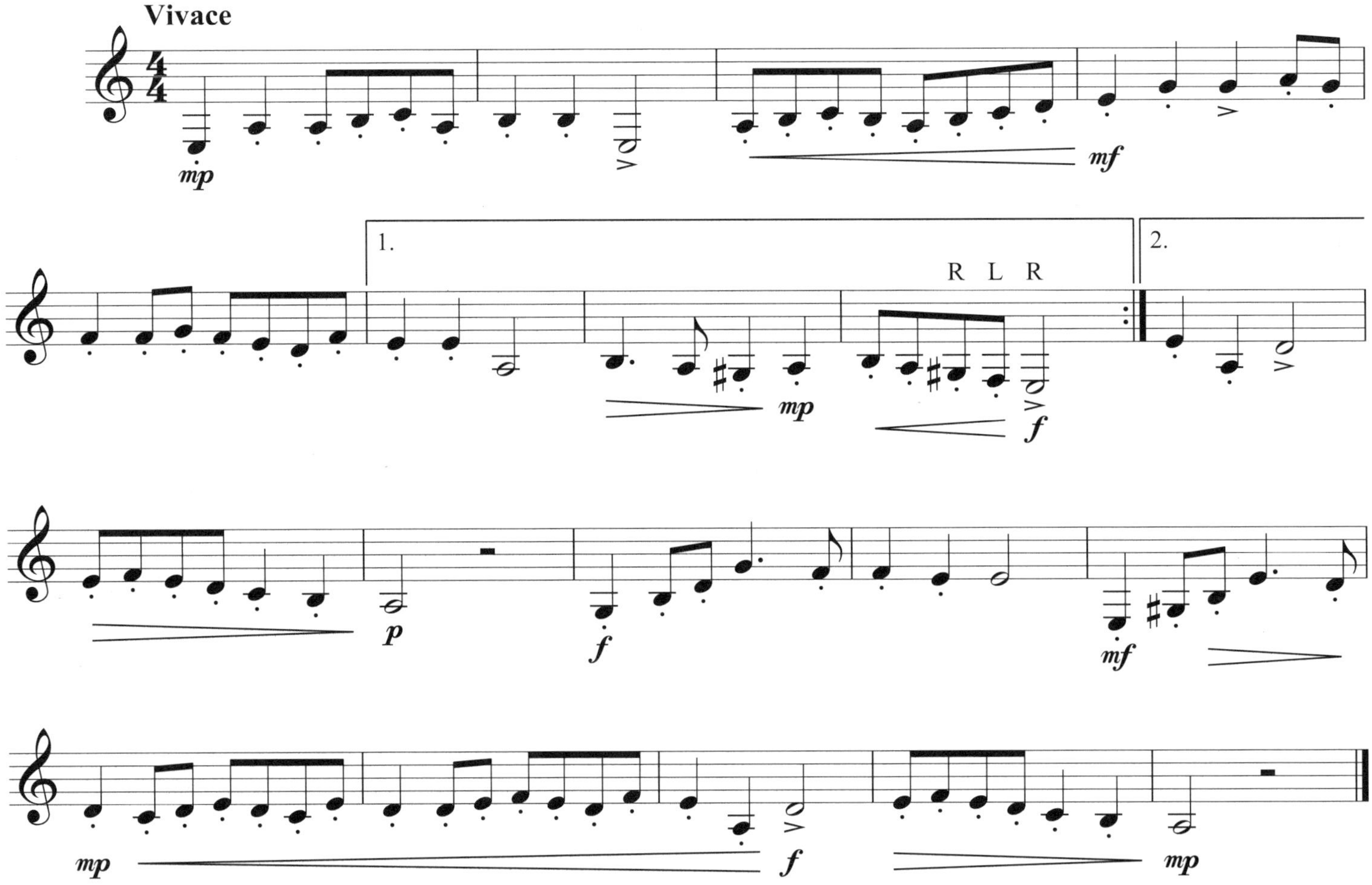
Vivace
mp
mf
1.
2.
R L R
mp
f
p
f
mf
mp
f
mp

**TOOLBOX**

**2/4 Time**

**2** = 2 beats in each measure
**4** = A quarter note receives one beat

# ALL JOIN HANDS

Game Song

**TOOLBOX**

**Sixteenth Rest**
A sixteenth rest is worth one-quarter of a beat.

**Dotted Eighth Rest**
A dotted eighth rest is worth three-quarters of a beat.

Eighth Rest + Sixteenth Rest = Dotted Eighth Rest

# KARMA CHAMELEON

Words and Music by George O'Dowd, Jonathan Moss, Michael Craig, Roy Hay and Phil Pickett

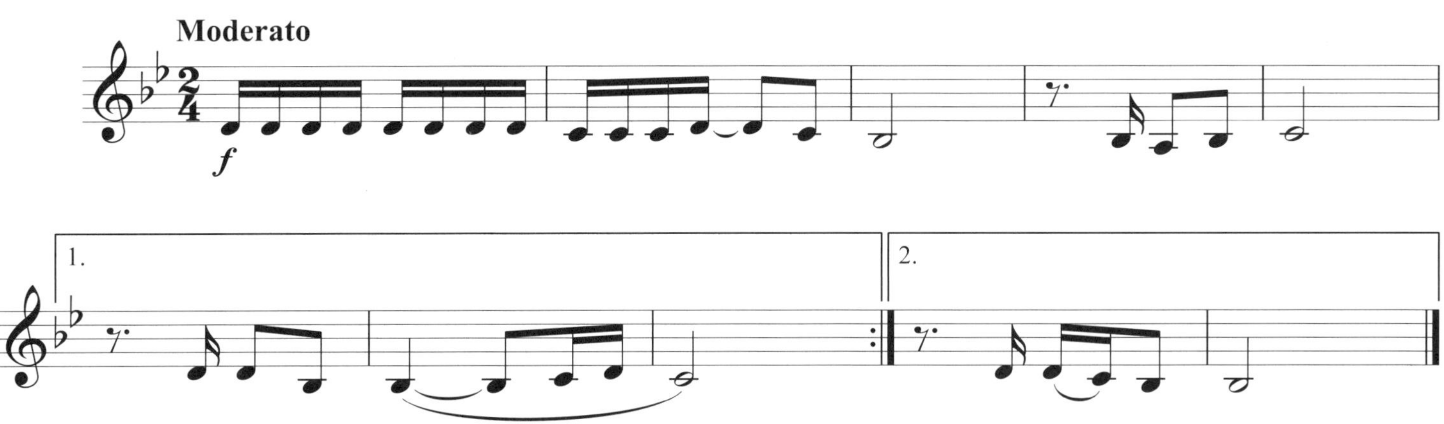

In "Finale" from the *William Tell Overture*, you will hear 7 clicks on the recording before the pickup note to bar 1.

# DUET: FINALE

## from William Tell Overture

By Gioachino Rossini

f
f

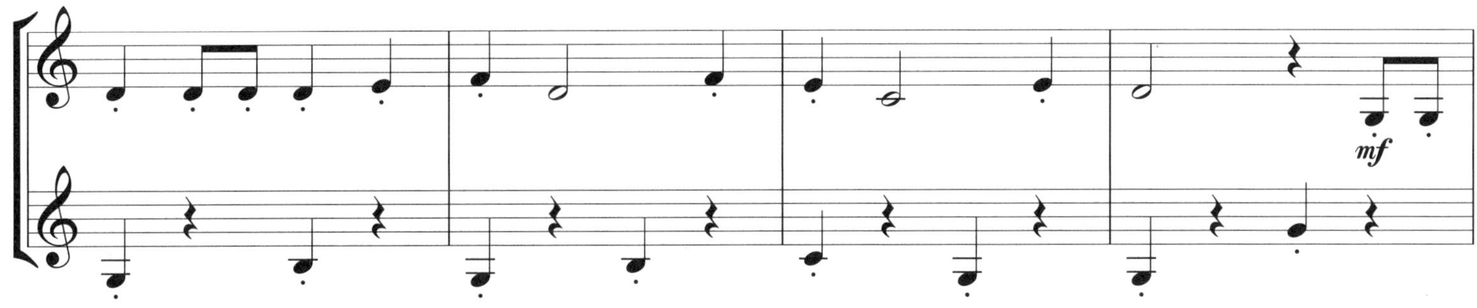
mf

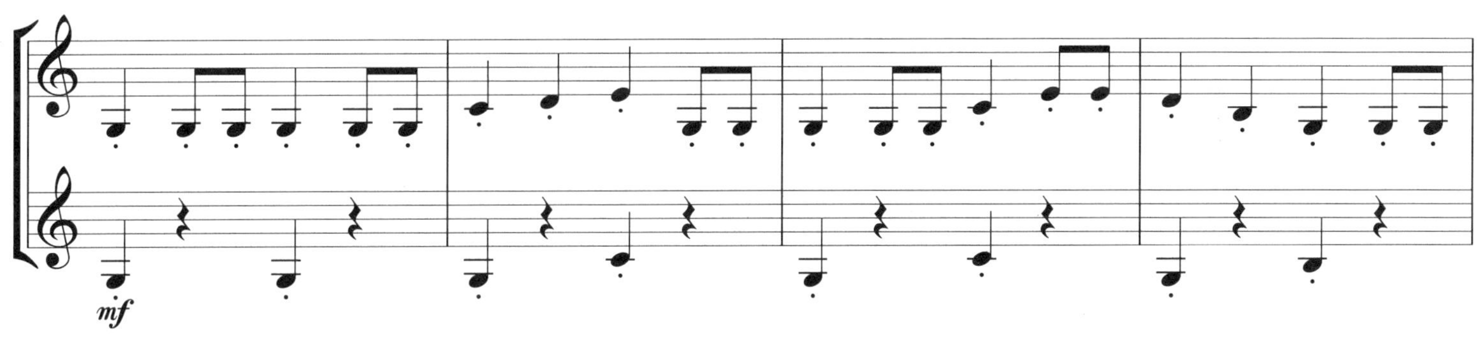
mf

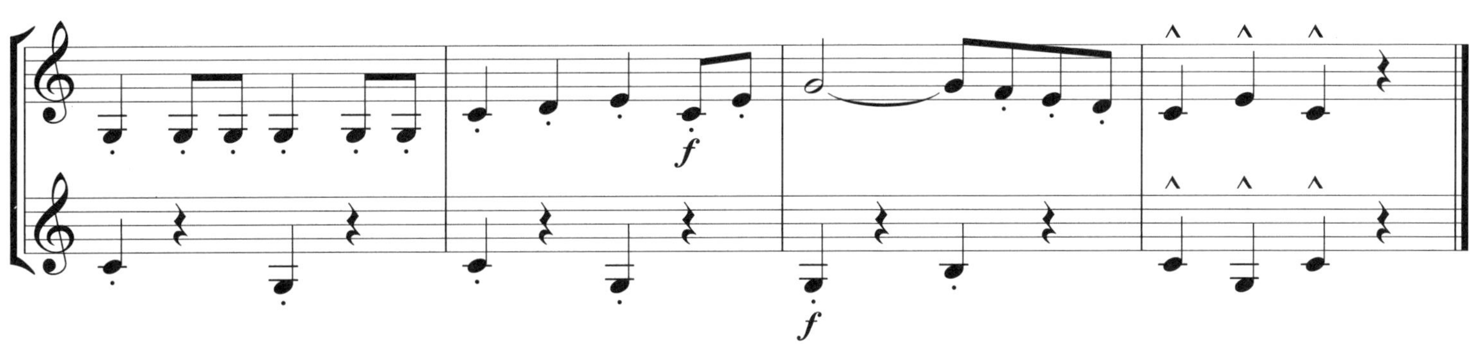
f
f

# LESSON 9:
## The Clarion Register

### New Notes

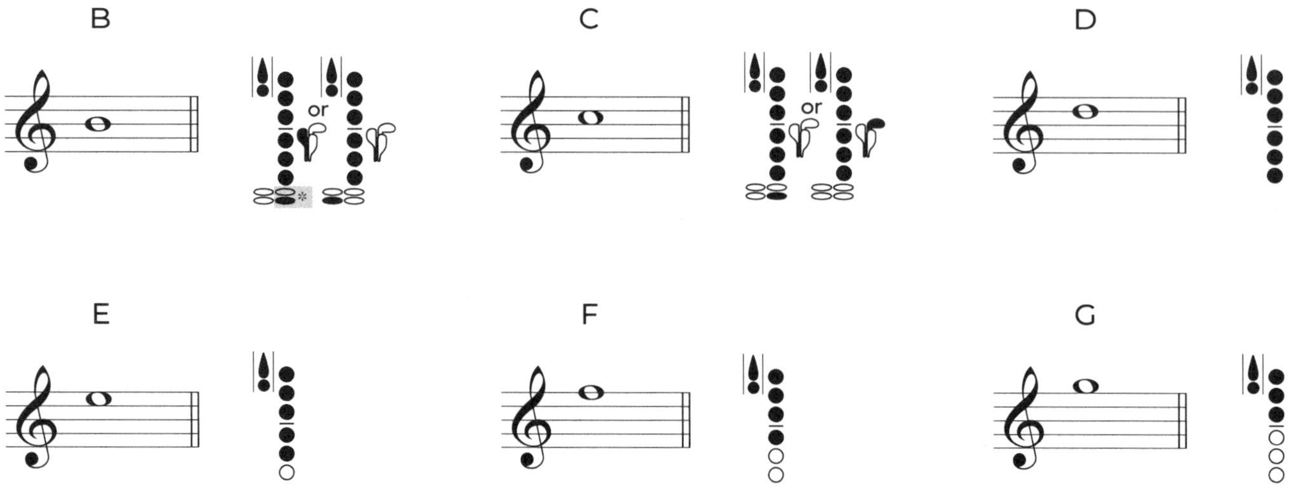


* B should be played with just your left pinky. However, sometimes you need to add the F/C key if your clarinet is out of adjustment

All the notes you have been playing so far represent the lowest-sounding notes on the clarinet. Adding the key above your thumb, the *register key*, takes you into a higher range of notes, the *clarion register*. Watch the video to learn about proper air, embouchure, and fingering techniques to make this easier.

These high notes are much more sensitive to weak air, so keep your air stream fast, strong, and steady. For most people, the high notes are easier with a slightly more resistant reed, so you may be outgrowing your beginner reed. The ideal strength for you depends upon your equipment, but for most people, the clarion register is easier with a reed that is at least 2.5 or stronger.

### Left-Hand Thumb Placement

Place your left thumb so it always slightly touches the register key whenever it covers the thumb hole. Move your thumb and hand as little as possible. Your thumb needs to cover the thumb hole when you press down the register key. This will change your low note into a note that is twelve notes higher.

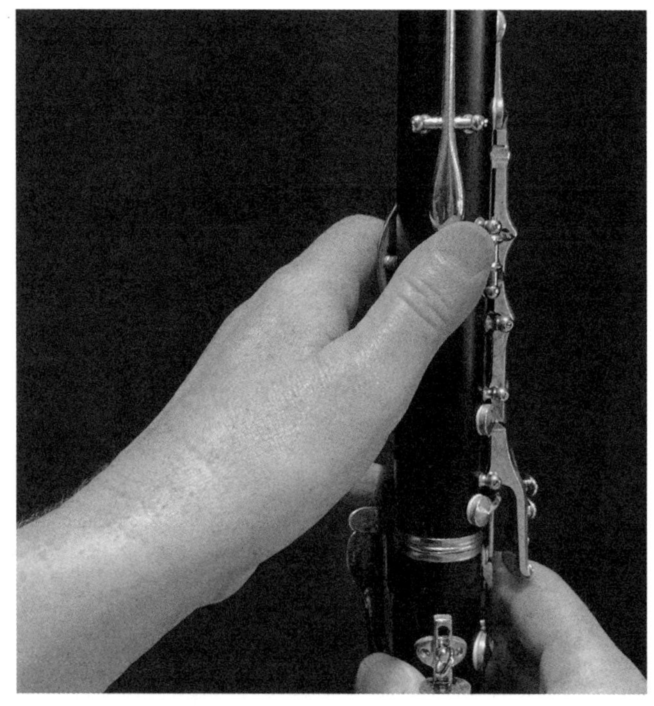

In "Leaping Lizards," each pair of notes has the same fingering, but the second note has the added register key.

### Leaping Lizards

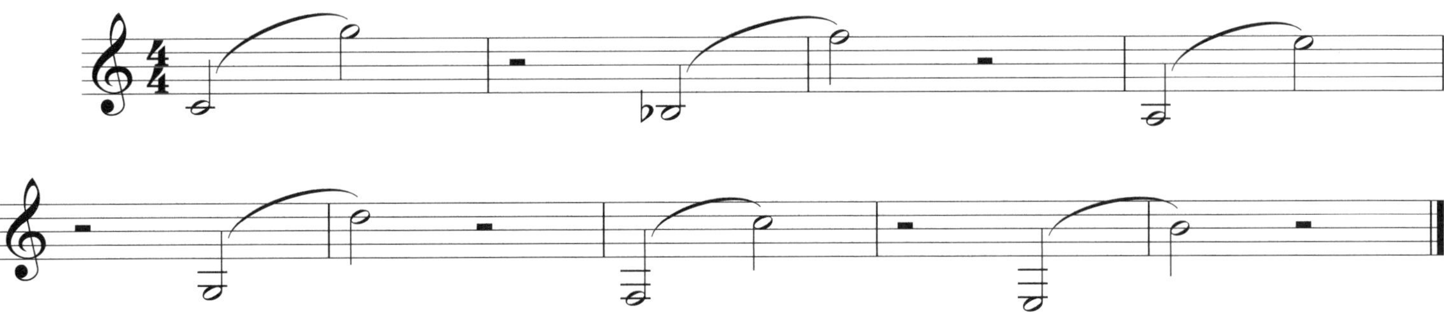

### Steppin' Up to E

**TOOLBOX**

**D.C. al fine**
D.C. is an abbreviation for *Da Capo*, which means go back to the beginning. *Al fine* means that once you repeat from the start, play until you see a final bar line 𝄂 with the word *Fine*, which is the end.

## FAIS DO-DO (GO TO SLEEP)

Traditional French Lullaby

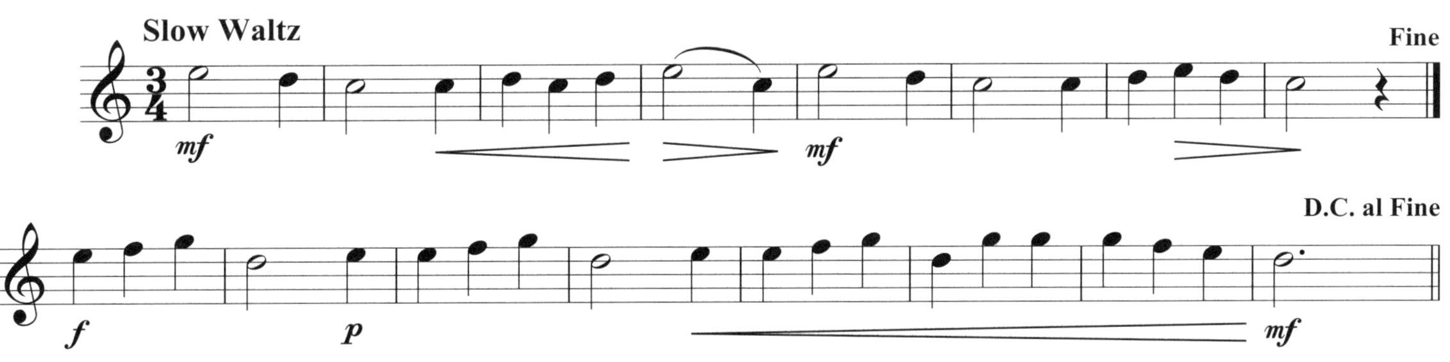




**CLARINET TALK**

Remember to tongue with a "tee" syllable at the tip of the reed and that higher notes require a faster air speed.

The following version of "Ode to Joy" uses the same notes played earlier in the book but are an *octave* higher. An octave is the distance between two notes that are the same pitch and eight note names apart.

# ODE TO JOY

Music by Ludwig van Beethoven

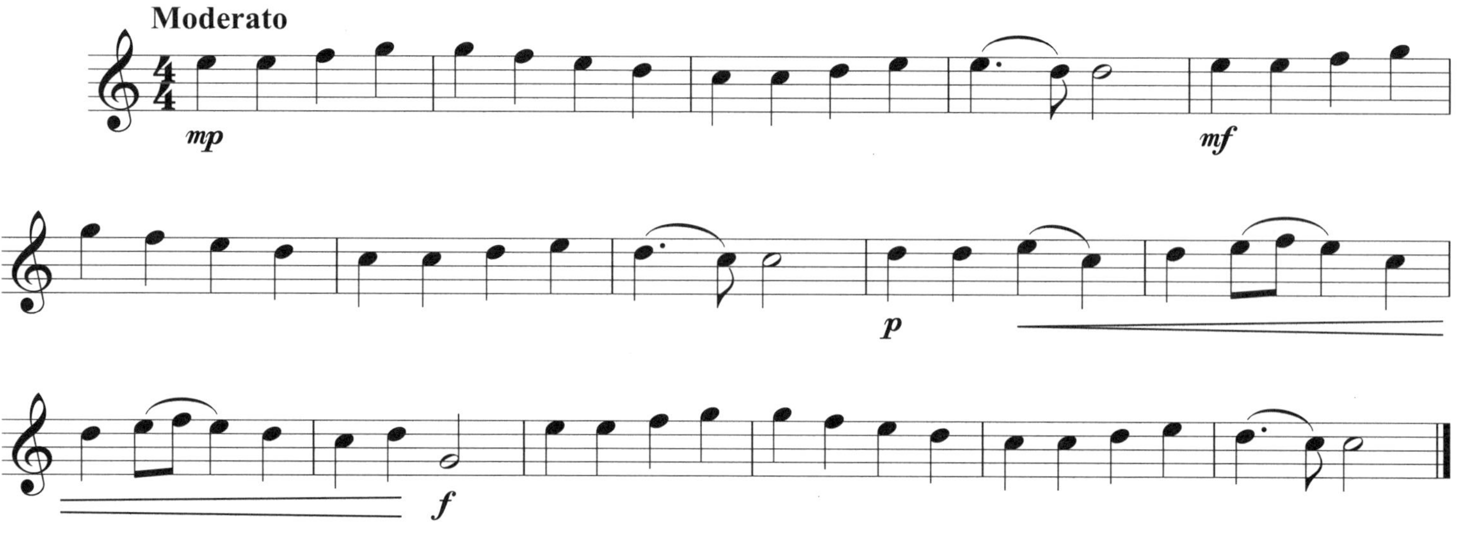




## Playin' Up High

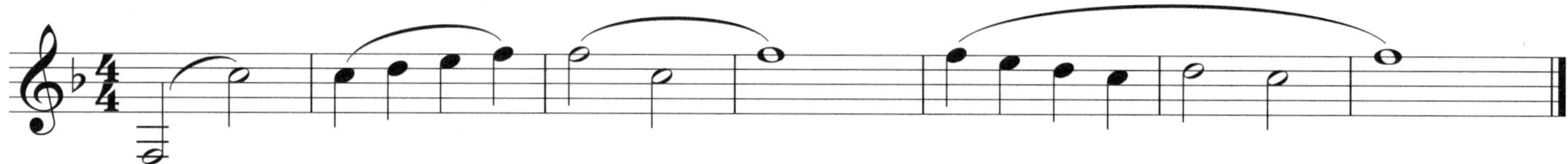

## B Limber

# MARY AND MARTHA

African American Folk Song

# TURN! TURN! TURN! (TO EVERYTHING THERE IS A SEASON)

Words from the Book of Ecclesiastes
Adaptation and Music by Pete Seeger

# COME SAIL AWAY

Words and Music by Dennis DeYoung

Forward to F

# BYE BYE LOVE

Words and Music by Felice Bryant and Boudleaux Bryant

Cee Gees

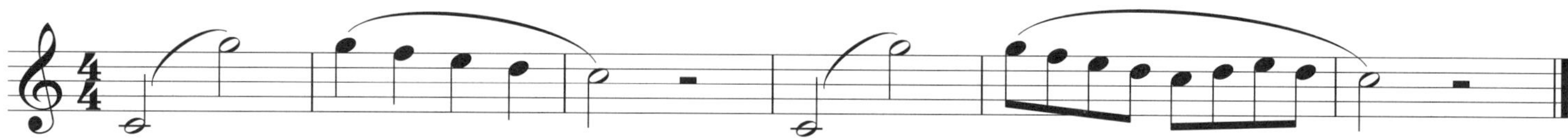

# DOWNTOWN

Words and Music by Tony Hatch

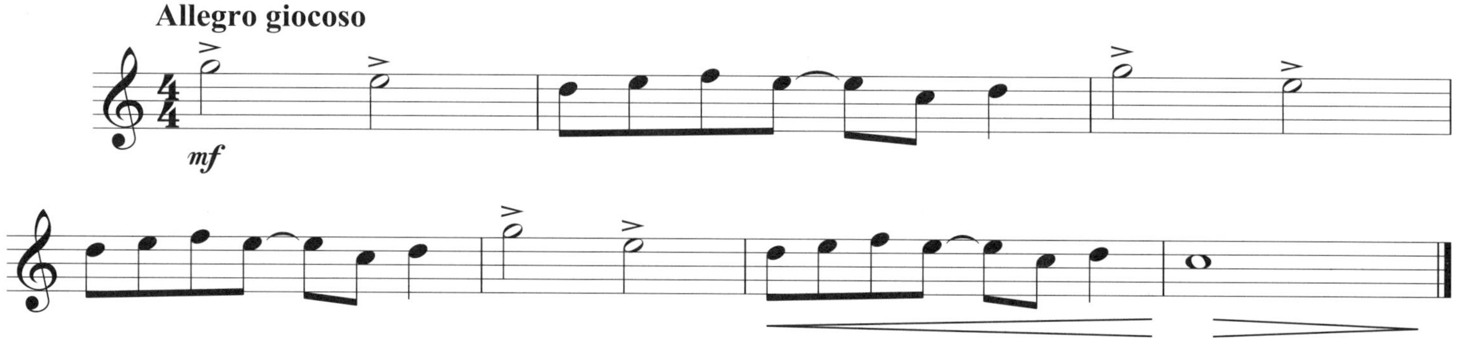

# FIREWORK

Words and Music by Katy Perry, Mikkel Eriksen, Tor Erik Hermansen, Esther Dean and Sandy Wilhelm

# ONE CALL AWAY

Words and Music by Charlie Puth, Justin Franks, Breyan Isaac, Matt Prime, Blake Anthony Carter and Maureen McDonald

Andante

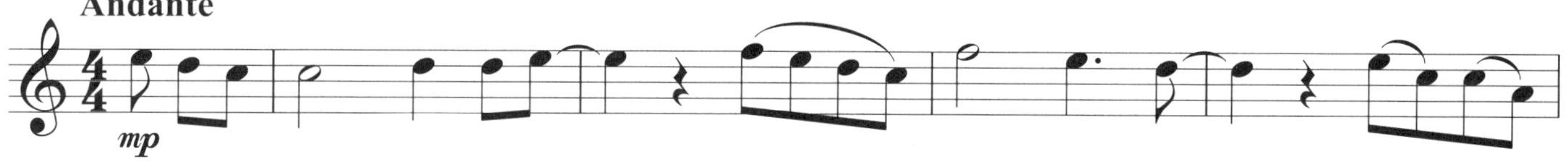

# DANCE MONKEY

Words and Music by Toni Watson

**TOOLBOX**

**D.S. al Coda**

D.S. is the abbreviation for *Del Segno* (the sign). When you reach the D.S. al Coda, return to the Del Segno (𝄋) and play until you reach the "To Coda" marking in the music. Then, jump to the *Coda* (𝄌), which is usually near the end of the piece, and play to the end.

# DUET: LINUS AND LUCY

## from A CHARLIE BROWN CHRISTMAS

By Vince Guaraldi

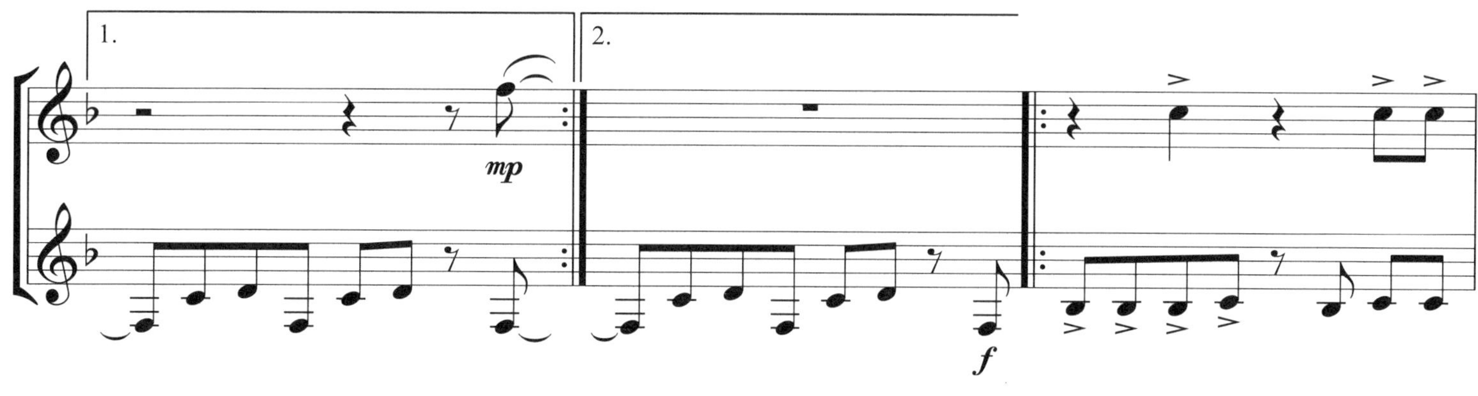
1.
2.
mp
f

Play 3 times
D.S. al Coda
mp

CODA
p
p

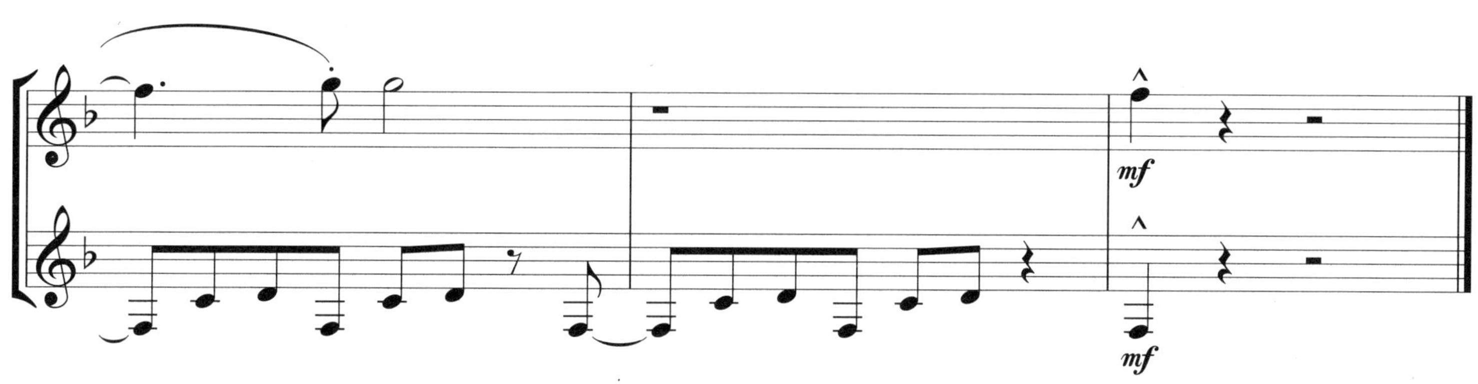
mf
mf

# LESSON 10:
## Connecting the Registers

We now know how to use our register key from the lower register (chalumeau) to the upper register (clarion). Next, we need to work on the techniques that help us connect the registers, also known as crossing *the break*.

### Tips for Success

1. Roll the left index finger onto the A key.
2. Always keep your fingers close to the keys.
3. Use the concept ***Right Hand Down*** (RHD). Right Hand Down means to keep the tone holes and the Low F/C key closed with right-hand fingers. Crossing the break will be easier and smoother since we only need to move our left-hand fingers. The only notes this may be used on are G, G♯/A♭, A, and A♯/B♭. These are also known as *throat tones*.

#### Smoothly Up and Over

#### Rolling to A

#### A Loopy Loops

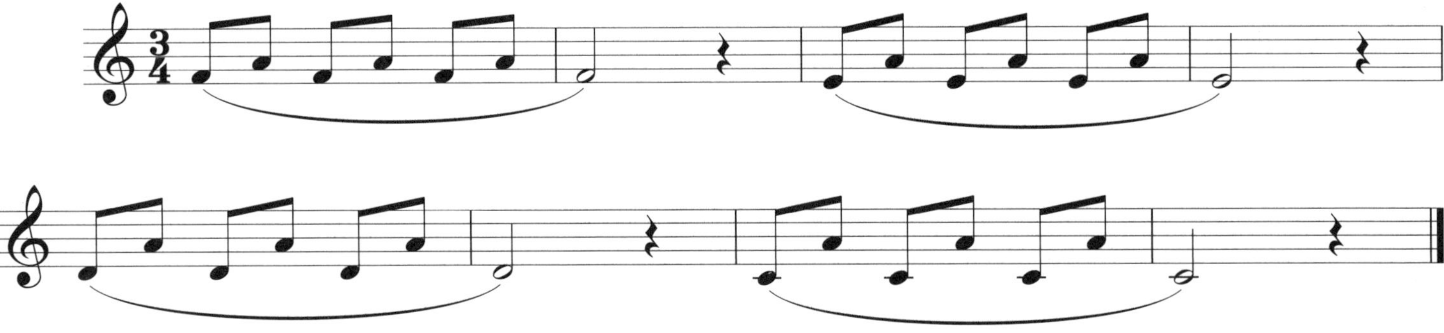

#### B-Flat Loopy Loops

### B-Flat Challenge Loopy Loops

## Notes for the Smooth Bees Exercise

It is helpful to practice the hand movements while holding the clarinet on your shoulder, by watching yourself in a mirror, or by recording a video of yourself. Roll your left index finger onto the A key while keeping the other left-hand fingers close to their tone holes. Concentrate on moving all your fingers together. Float the thumb over the tone hole on the back of the clarinet. Keep all four fingers of your right hand down during this process (RHD). Play with your best tone quality, maintaining a strong, beautiful sound and keep your embouchure stable. Remember to keep your air blowing across the break. Our natural instinct is to stop blowing or tongue the notes in order to hide finger slips.

### Smooth Bees

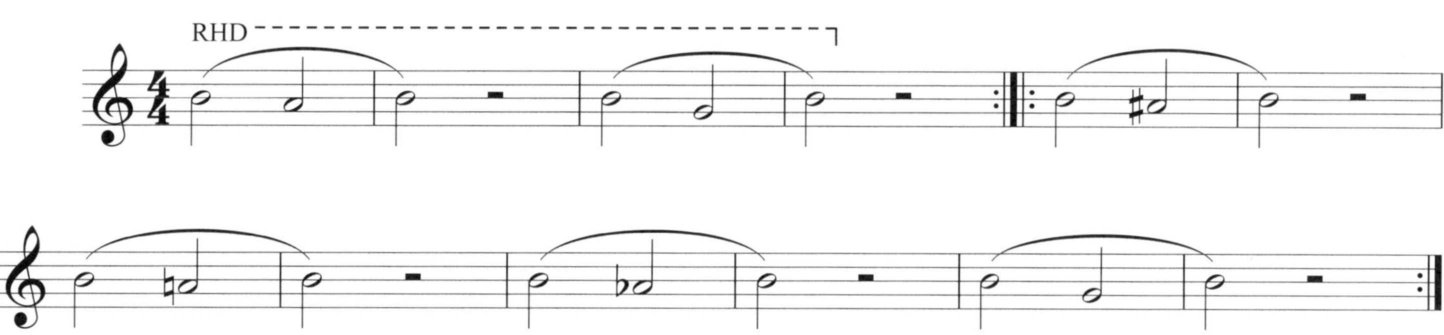


### Smooth Cees

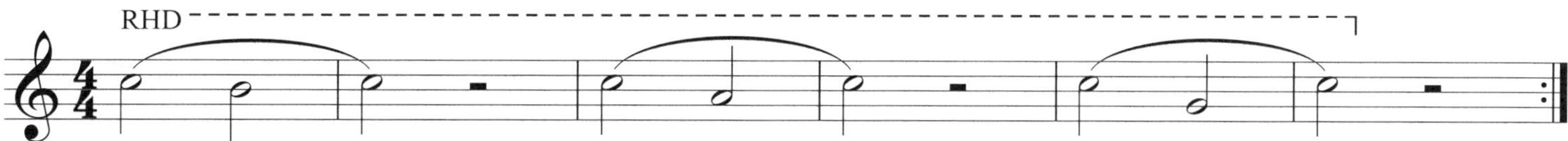


### Cee the Loopy Loops

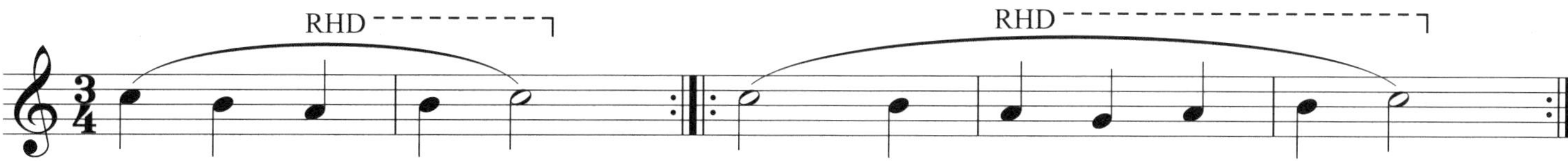

Staying Connected

# BRIDGE OVER TROUBLED WATER

Words and Music by Paul Simon

# LEAVING OF LIVERPOOL

Irish Sea Chanty

## New Note: F-Sharp/G-Flat

# THEME FROM "JURASSIC PARK"

from the Universal Motion Picture JURASSIC PARK

Composed by John Williams

# SHEPHERD'S HEY

English Folk Song

Smoother Cees

# EDELWEISS

from THE SOUND OF MUSIC

Lyrics by Oscar Hammerstein II

Music by Richard Rodgers

# MAKE NEW FRIENDS

Traditional

## New Note: D-Sharp/E-Flat

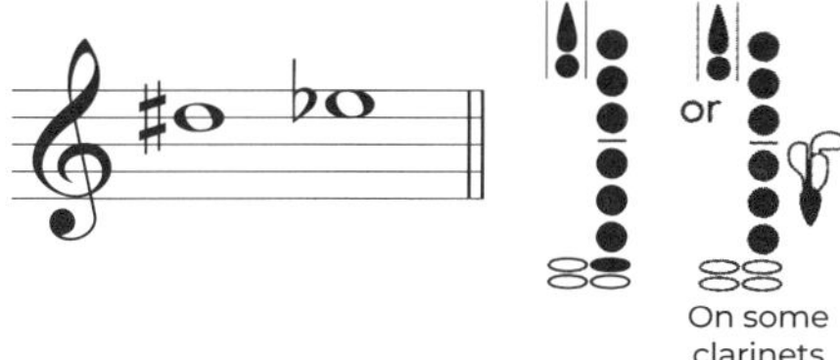


# ANTI-HERO

Words and Music by Taylor Swift and Jack Antonoff

## New Note: C-Sharp/D-Flat

C-sharp uses the same pinky keys as low F-sharp.

## Loopy Loops in C-Sharp

CLARINET TALK

**Creating Loopy Loops**

When a section of music is especially challenging, create your own Loopy Loops. Start by isolating the notes that are challenging, making each note the same length. Then, practice with the correct rhythm as a loop. Once it feels more comfortable, play the whole song.

# LIFT ME UP

## From Black Panther: Wakanda Forever

Words and Music by Robyn Fenty, Temilade Openiyi, Ludwig Göransson and Ryan Coogler

## Common Time and Cut Time

*Common time* is another name for 4/4 time. A **C** is sometimes used in our music instead of $\frac{4}{4}$. In 2/2 time—also known as *cut time*—there are two beats in a bar, and a half note gets one beat. A **₵** can be used in our music instead of $\frac{2}{2}$.

Compared to 4/4, it is as though every note value is cut in half. This is used to achieve a smoother feel in the music or to make the music look cleaner. Although you can think of cut time as a fast 4/4, it is useful to train yourself to think in two. The example below shows the same notes in 4/4 and 2/2 and how we would count each one.

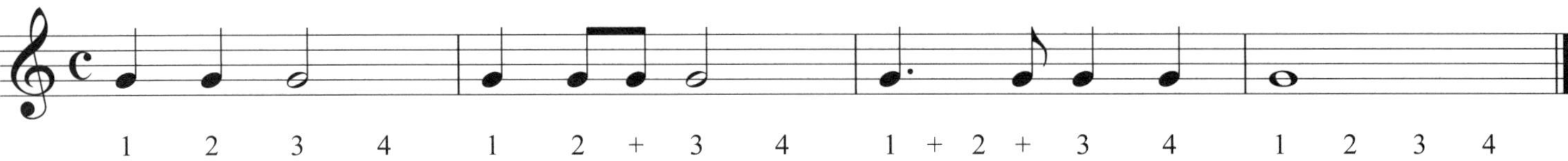

## Cut Time Training

# OB-LA-DI, OB-LA-DA

Words and Music by John Lennon and Paul McCartney

TOOLBOX

**D.C. al Coda**

Remember, D.C. is an abbreviation for *Da Capo*, which means go back to the beginning. This is usually followed by *al Fine* (play to the *Fine* mark and stop) or *al Coda* (jump to the Coda symbol ⊕ and play to the end).

# NOWHERE MAN

Words and Music by John Lennon and Paul McCartney

# A DREAM IS A WISH YOUR HEART MAKES

from CINDERELLA

Music by Mack David and Al Hoffman

Lyrics by Jerry Livingston

## New Note: A

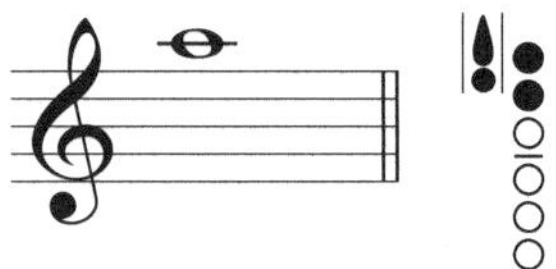

# DUET: ANDANTE GRAZIOSO

from PIANO SONATA IN A MAJOR

By Wolfgang Amadeus Mozart

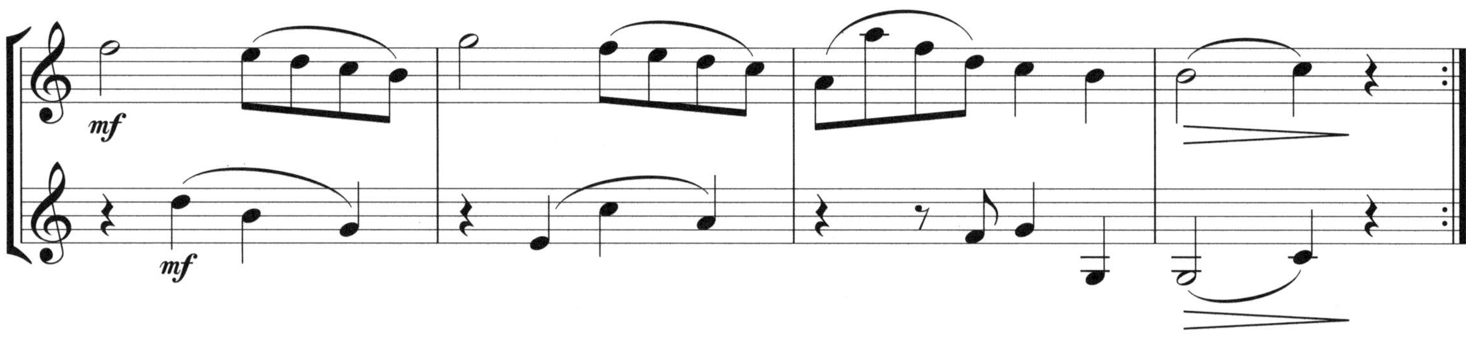

# LESSON 11:
## Tempo Changes

TOOLBOX

**Ritardando**
*Ritardando* (*ritard.* or *rit.)* means to slow down gradually.

### BEAUTY AND THE BEAST
from BEAUTY AND THE BEAST
Music by Alan Menken
Lyrics by Howard Ashman

TOOLBOX

**Fermata** 𝄐
A *fermata* is a dramatic pause in the music. Often, a fermata approximately doubles a note length. If you are playing with an ensemble, hold the note as the conductor instructs.

TOOLBOX

**Accelerando**
*Accelerando* (*accel.*) means to speed up gradually.

# ITSY BITSY TEENIE WEENIE YELLOW POLKA DOT BIKINI

Words and Music by Paul Vance and Lee Pockriss

Allegro
RHD
mf
accel.
RHD



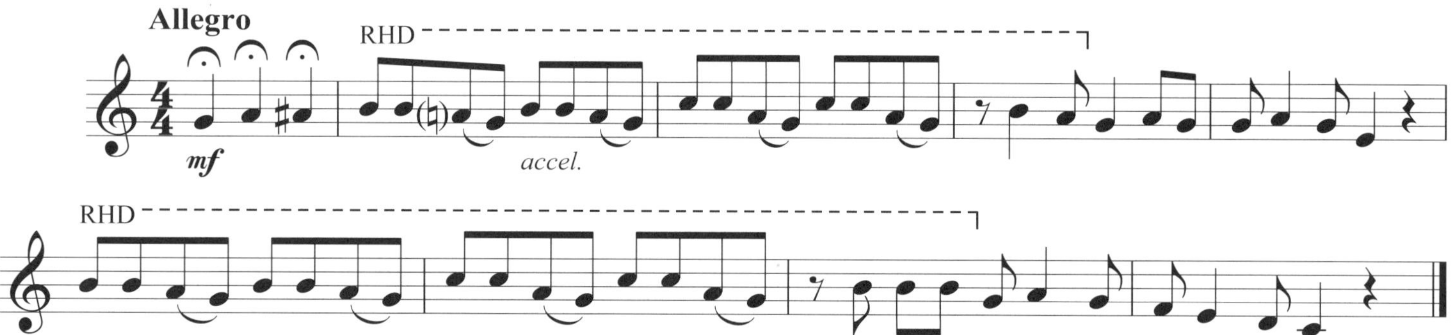

# YESTERDAY

Words and Music by John Lennon and Paul McCartney

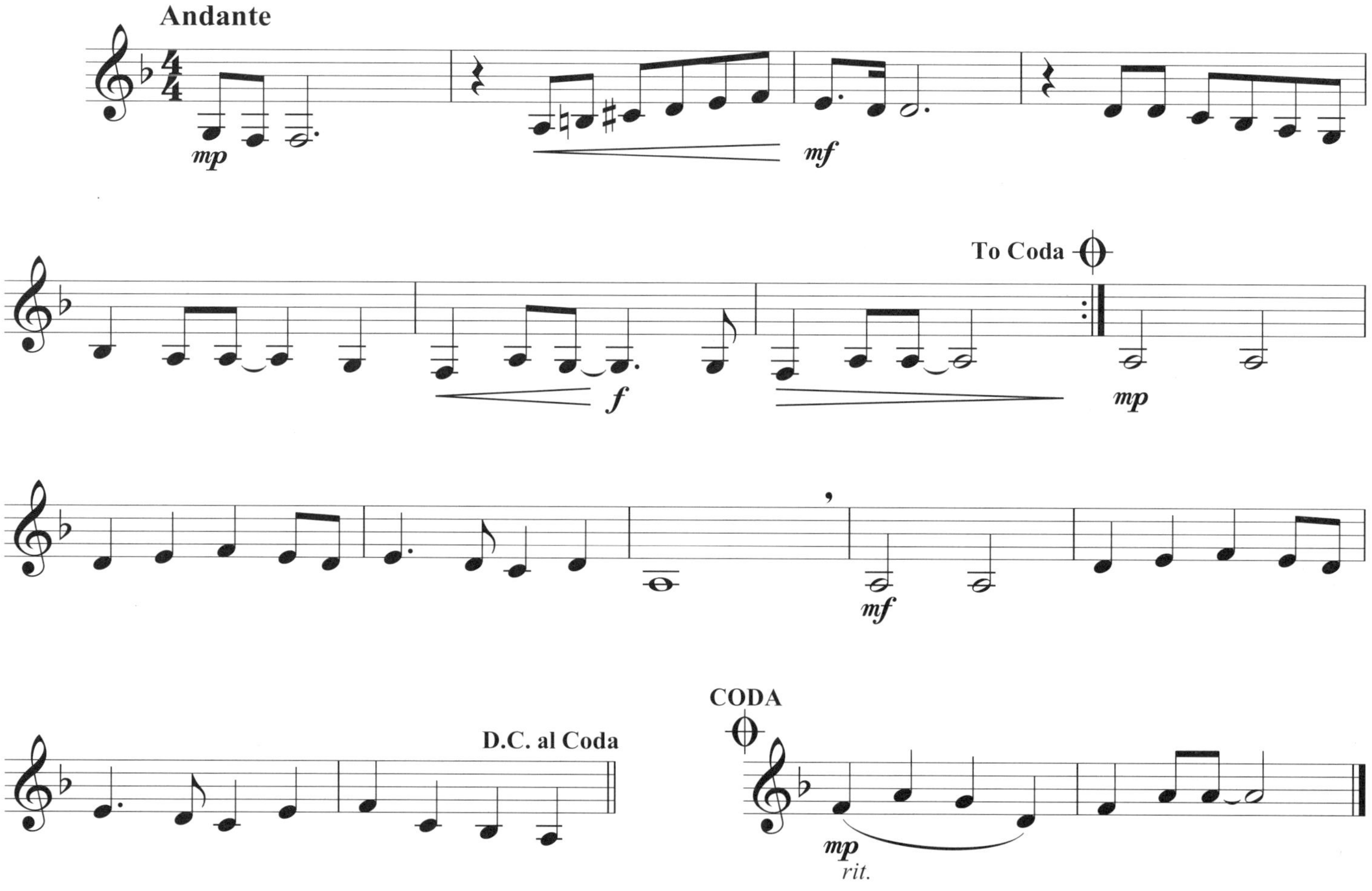
Andante
mp
mf
To Coda
f
mp
mf
D.C. al Coda
CODA
mp
rit.

In "Chromatic Patterns Clarion," notice that lines one and two are identical fingerings, except that line two adds the register key.

### Chromatic Patterns Clarion

### More Leaping Lizards

Remember to use RHD to keep the connections smooth.

### B-Break Loops

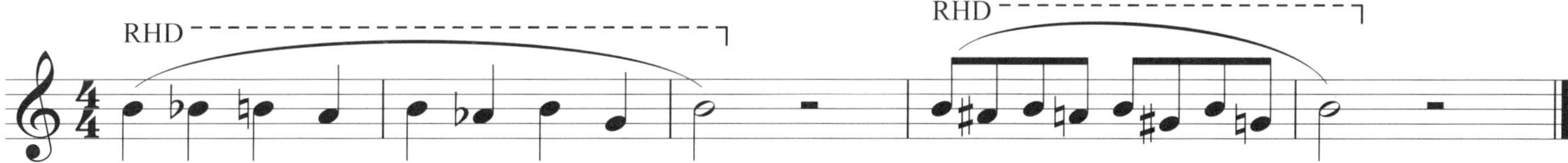


Sometimes, we need our tongue to move quickly, such as tonguing sixteenth notes at a fast tempo, as found in "Pick-A-Little, Talk-A-Little." Touch the reed lightly with the tip of the tongue (do not hammer). Keep the tip of the tongue as close to the reed as possible while maintaining a fast and steady airflow. Refer to the tonguing videos in Lessons 1 and 8 before practicing this song.

# PICK-A-LITTLE, TALK-A-LITTLE/ GOODNIGHT LADIES

from Meredith Willson's THE MUSIC MAN

By Meredith Willson

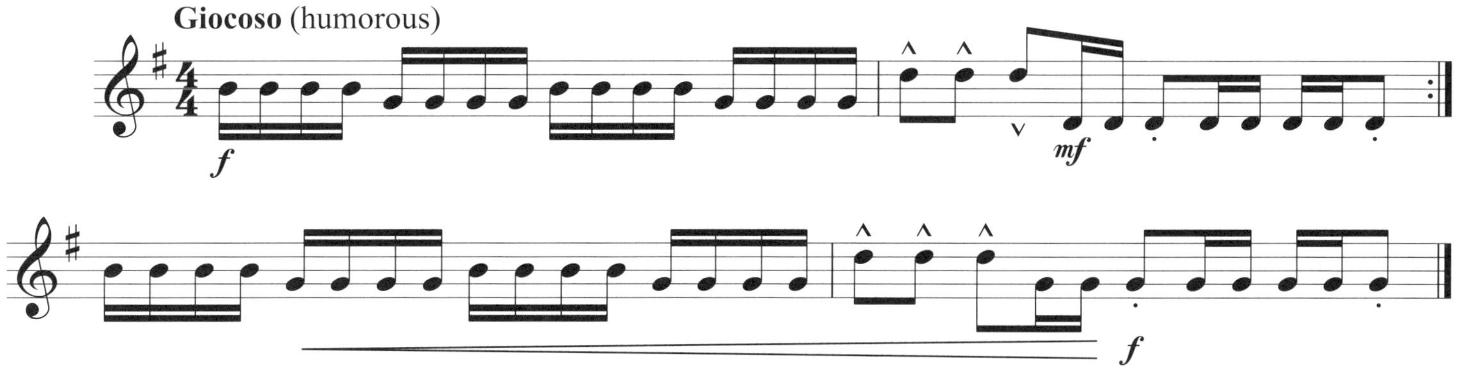

C How Easy It Is

Loopy Loops B-Flat

Loopy Loops in F

C These Chromatic Loops

# WHEN THE SAINTS GO MARCHING IN

Traditional

## New Note: G-Sharp/A-flat

### Moving Up!

### Left C to Right E-Flat Exercise

# YOU BELONG WITH ME

Words and Music by Taylor Swift and Liz Rose

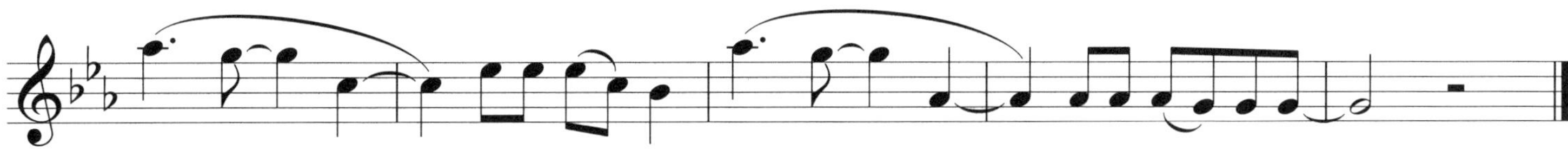

**TOOLBOX**

**D.S. al Fine**
Remember, D.S. is an abbreviation for *Del Segno*, which means to go back to the sign (𝄋). This is usually followed by *al Fine* (play to the *Fine* mark and stop) or *al Coda* (jump to the Coda symbol 𝄌 and play to the end).

**TOOLBOX**

**A Tempo**
*A tempo* means to go back to the speed you were at previously.

# WHISTLE WHILE YOU WORK

## from SNOW WHITE AND THE SEVEN DWARFS

Words by Larry Morey
Music by Frank Churchill

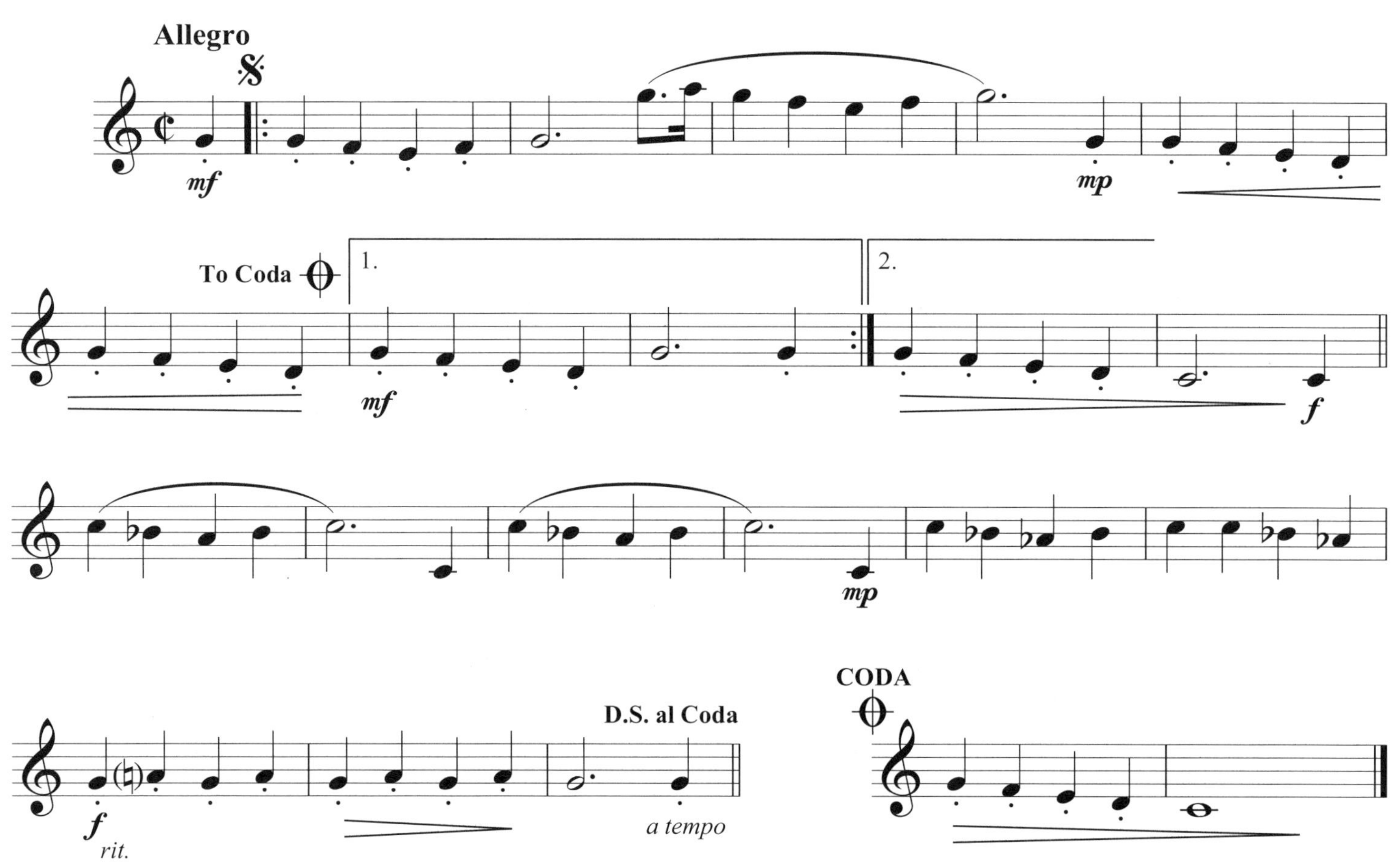

## Musical Styles

When we perform music of different styles, we can portray the mood of the music differently by changing our articulation, note length, dynamics, timbre (tone color), and more. Slow, expressive pieces often have very connected notes with legato articulation. Fast and lively songs may have more distinct, clear articulation and often shorter notes. Jazz and Swing styles use a very light articulation, and rhythmically, the on-beat eighth notes are worth two-thirds of a beat, while off-beat eighths get the remaining third for a jazz pulse. This lesson gives you many genres to explore, and the accompanying video gives style suggestions for this music.

# THE MUSIC OF THE NIGHT

### from THE PHANTOM OF THE OPERA

Music by Andrew Lloyd Webber
Lyrics by Charles Hart
Additional Lyrics by Richard Stilgoe

# ARE YOU LONESOME TONIGHT?

Words and Music by Roy Turk and Lou Handman

# ROCK AROUND THE CLOCK

Words and Music by Max C. Freedman and Jimmy DeKnight

**TOOLBOX**

**Feeling $\frac{3}{4}$ in 1**

When songs have a quicker tempo in 3/4, we often refer to the tempo as being felt "in one." So, instead of three beats per measure, there is one large pulse that we internally subdivide into three lesser beats. Set your metronome at a speed where each click equals a dotted half note. When playing, place a greater emphasis on the first beat of each measure, as you would feel in a waltz.

# MY FAVORITE THINGS

## from THE SOUND OF MUSIC

Lyrics by Oscar Hammerstein II

Music by Richard Rodgers

# PIANO MAN

Words and Music by Billy Joel

# THE STRIPPER

from THE STRIPPER

Music by David Rose

Loopy Loop Prep for Bibbidi-Bobbidi-Boo

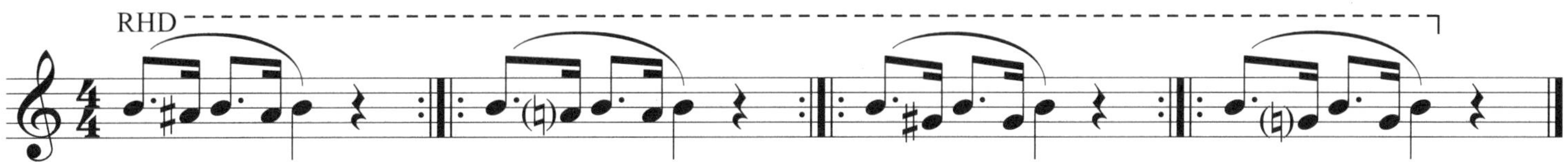


# BIBBIDI-BOBBIDI-BOO (THE MAGIC SONG)

from CINDERELLA

Words by Jerry Livingston

Music by Mack David and Al Hoffman

## Loopy Loop Prep for Ain't Misbehavin'

Swing Eighths
3
R or
L
R L
L R L

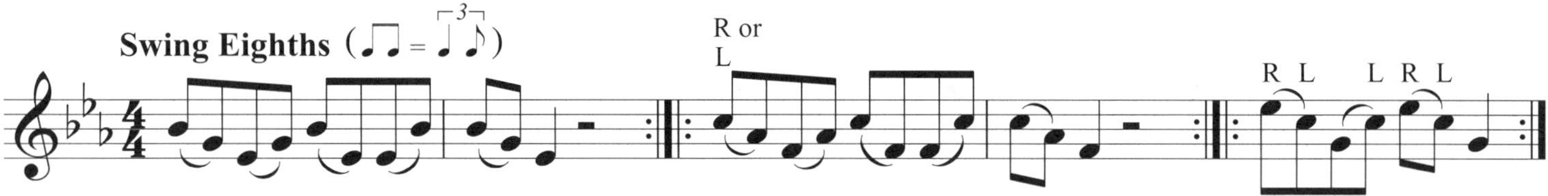

# AIN'T MISBEHAVIN'

Words by Andy Razaf
Music by Thomas "Fats" Waller and Harry Brooks

Easy Swing
3
mf
To Coda
1.
2.
f
L
ff
D.C. al Coda
CODA

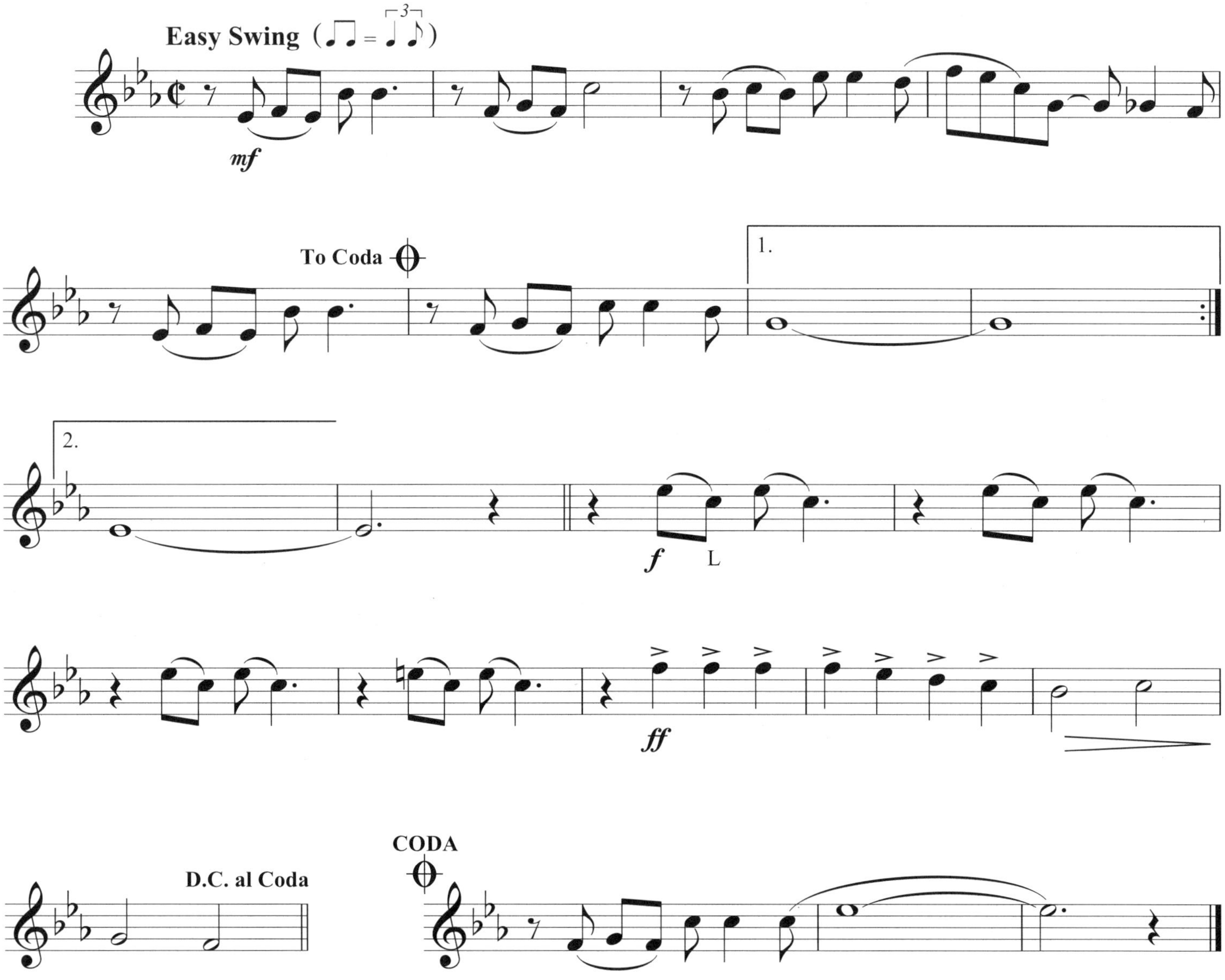

# STORMY WEATHER
# (KEEPS RAININ' ALL THE TIME)

from COTTON CLUB PARADE OF 1933
featured in the Motion Picture STORMY WEATHER

Words and Music by Ted Koehler and Harold Arlen

# DUET: WHEN I'M SIXTY-FOUR

Words and Music by John Lennon and Paul McCartney

D.S. al Coda
CODA

# LESSON 12:
# The Upper Clarion Register

As we move into higher notes on the clarinet, it is sometimes helpful to use a slightly stronger reed than you did as a beginner. A stronger reed allows you to use more air and have stronger embouchure support. You need to experiment to see what works for you, but generally, if you are using fast, steady air to support these high notes, a reed strength of at least three is preferred. A stronger reed allows you to use more air to produce a fuller sound.

We often don't think about what our tongue is doing when we are not tonguing. The position of the tongue has a huge influence on our tone and pitch. For a good classical tone, we want our tongue high in our mouth as if we are saying "hee." Having your tongue in this position will make the higher notes much easier to play. (See the video from Lesson 9 for a review of this.)

## New Notes

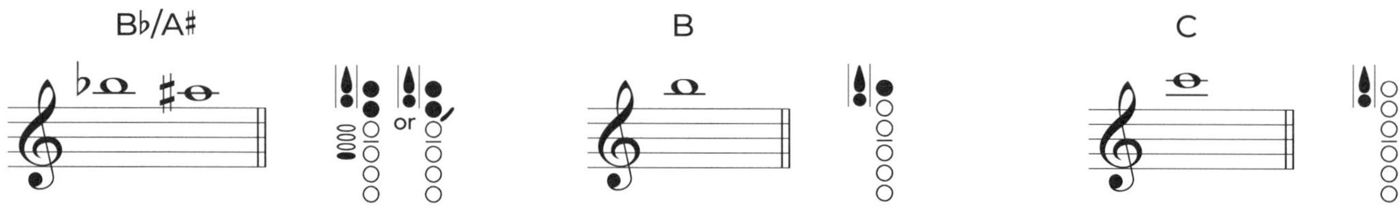


## Upper Clarion Loopy Loop

**TOOLBOX**

**Transposing Keys**
We first played "Love Me Tender" in Lesson 3. This version is *transposed* to a different key. When we transpose music, the distance between the notes is the same, but we start on a different pitch. Compare this version of "Love Me Tender" to the one learned in Lesson 3.

# LOVE ME TENDER

Words and Music by Elvis Presley and Vera Matson

# HE'S GOT THE WHOLE WORLD IN HIS HANDS

Traditional Spiritual

# EIGHT DAYS A WEEK

Words and Music by John Lennon and Paul McCartney

# THE LION SLEEPS TONIGHT

New Lyrics and Revised Music by George David Weiss, Luigi Creatore and Hugo Peretti

# BOUND FOR SOUTH AUSTRALIA

Australian Sea Chanty

# YAKETY YAK

Words and Music by Jerry Leiber and Mike Stoller

# ELEANOR RIGBY

Words and Music by John Lennon and Paul McCartney

p
mf
f
mp
f

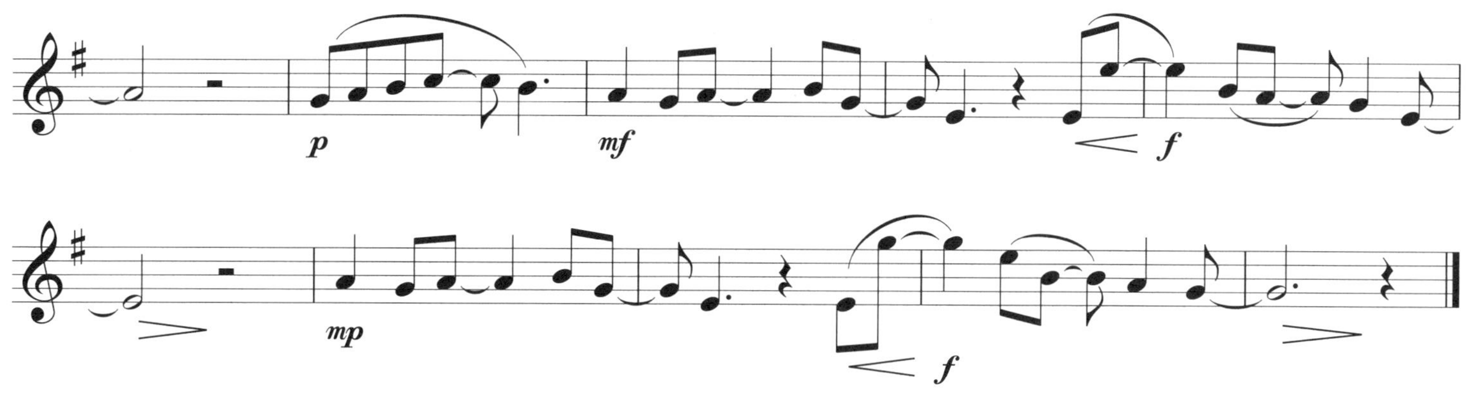

# DETROIT CITY

Words and Music by Danny Dill and Mel Tillis

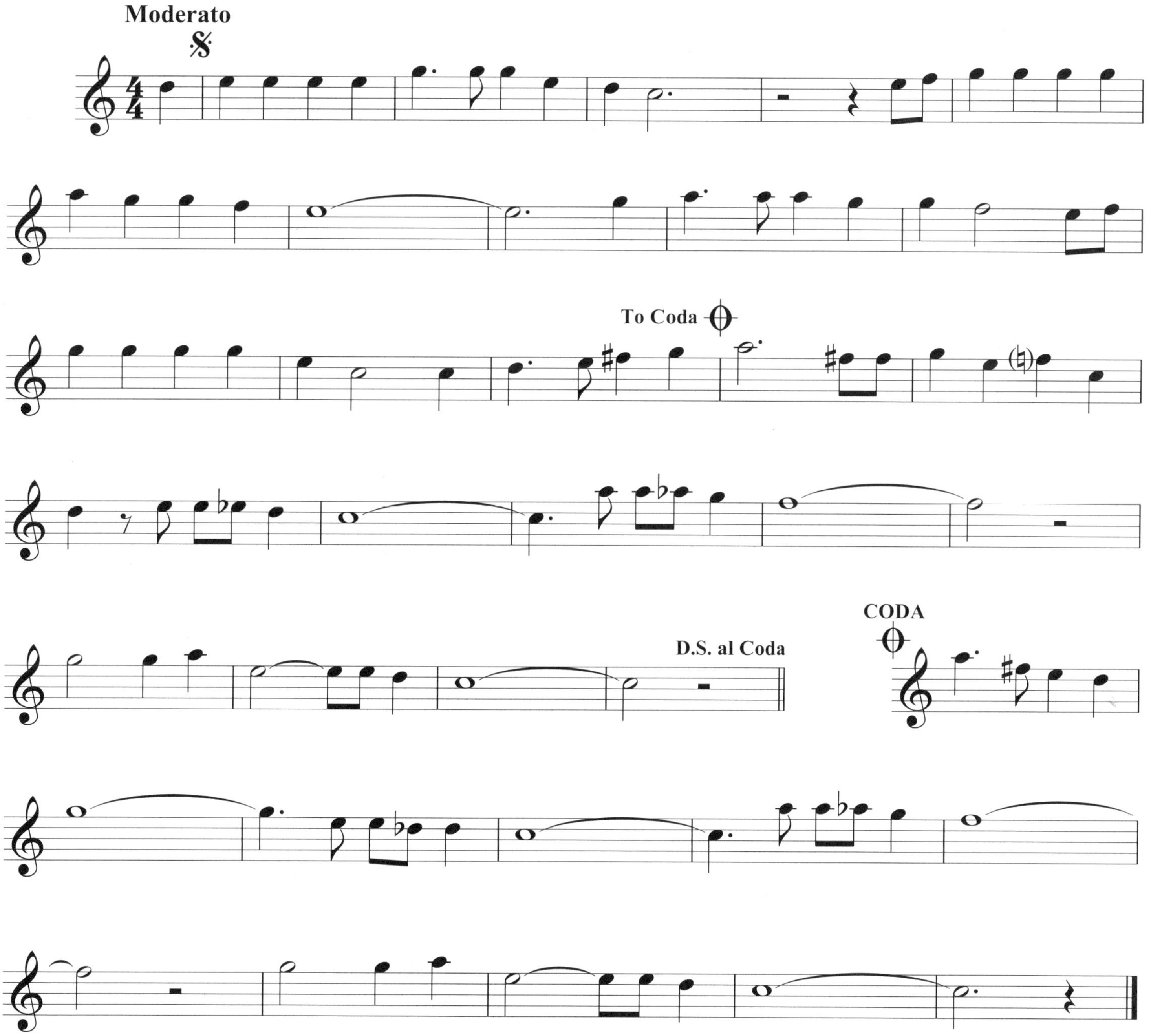
Moderato
To Coda
D.S. al Coda
CODA

# CANTINA BAND

## from STAR WARS: A NEW HOPE

Music by John Williams

TOOLBOX

**Grace Notes**

The tiny notes in the second bar of "Stranger on the Shore" are called grace notes. A grace note anticipates the note that it leads to, which will be played exactly in rhythm. It is like speaking "ta-da," where the "da" is the note that the grace note leads to. Grace notes are always tiny. We play them as quickly as possible before the next full sized note.

# STRANGER ON THE SHORE

## from FLAMINGO KID

Words by Robert Mellin
Music by Acker Bilk

**TOOLBOX**

**Legato**

*Legato* means to play smoothly. When playing the second clarinet part in "Air on a G String," make the notes as connected as possible while still tonguing each note.

# DUET: AIR ON A G STRING

## from ORCHESTRAL SUITE NO. 3 IN D MAJOR

By Johann Sebastian Bach

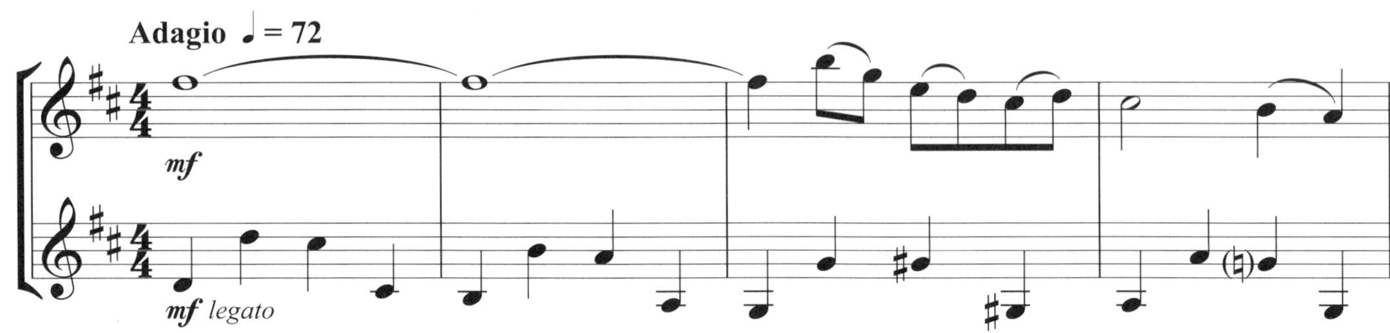


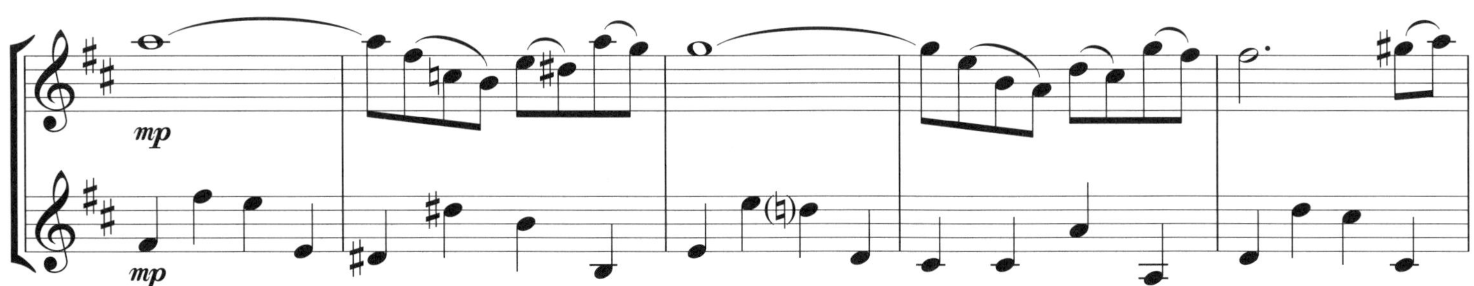

cresc.
cresc.
f
f
decresc.
decresc.
mp
mp
mf
mp

# LESSON 13:
# The Altissimo Register

## New Notes

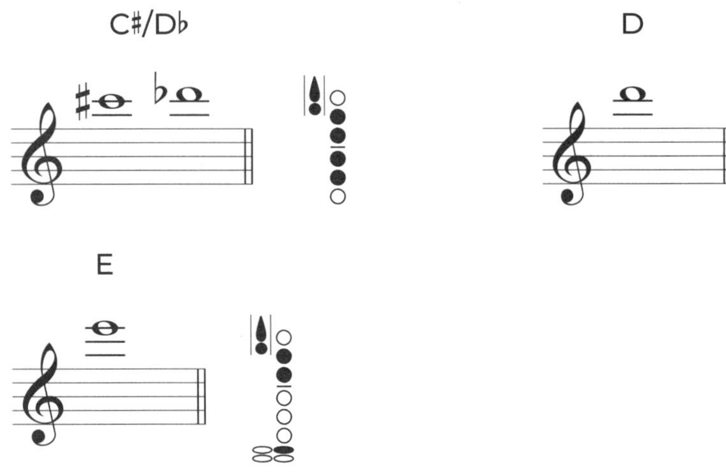


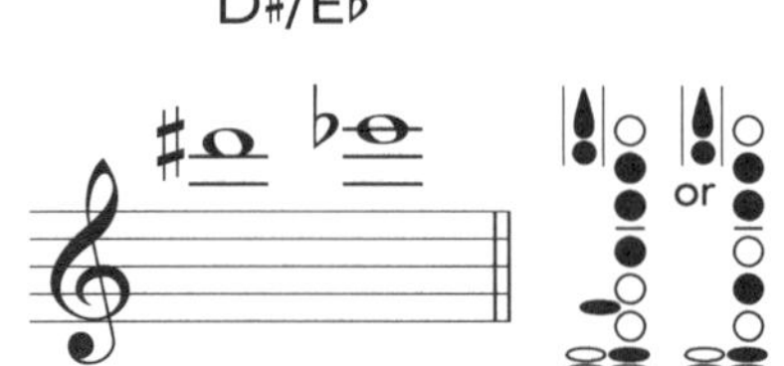


## Introduction to the Altissimo Register

The altissimo register uses the top hole on the upper joint (your left hand) as a register key. It allows the highest notes to sound on the clarinet, which we call the *altissimo* notes.

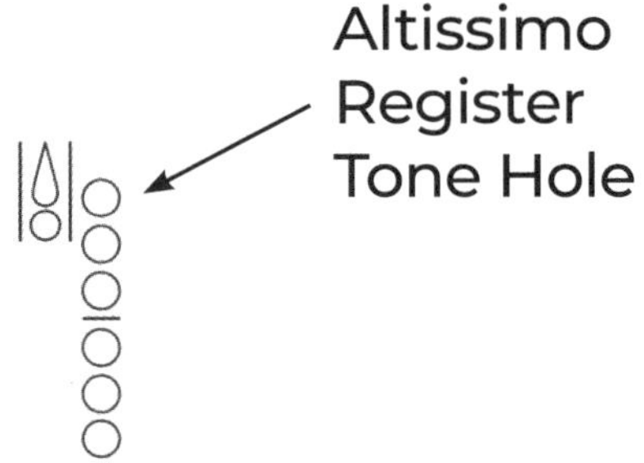


The easiest way to approach the altissimo notes is to start by using a lower fingering and going up to the altissimo register, as in the exercise "Stretching Our Limits."

1. Play low A with your best sound. When we add the register key, the A becomes the fourth space E.
2. Next, continue blowing and lift the left index finger. This tone hole acts as a second register key, and the altissimo C♯ will sound. Altissimo notes generally need a faster airstream than lower notes. If these notes don't sound, try a slightly harder reed and/or slightly more reed and mouthpiece in the mouth. Experiment to find the best position to create an optimal sound through all three clarinet registers.

CLARINET TALK

**Using a Half-Hole**

Lifting the top finger on our left hand acts as the register key to take us to the altissimo notes. This changes the air resistance in the clarinet and sometimes makes these notes feel like they pop out. An alternative to lifting your top index finger is to slide downward to open half of the tone hole. This can make the transition feel smoother, but it is a new fingering pattern to learn and may feel awkward at first. Either open-hole or half-hole is a good technique to approach the altissimo notes.

Beyond the altissimo C♯, you can see that part of the fingering is using the E♭ helper key with our right pinky. All notes above altissimo C♯ will require the use of the E♭ helper key to make the notes in tune.

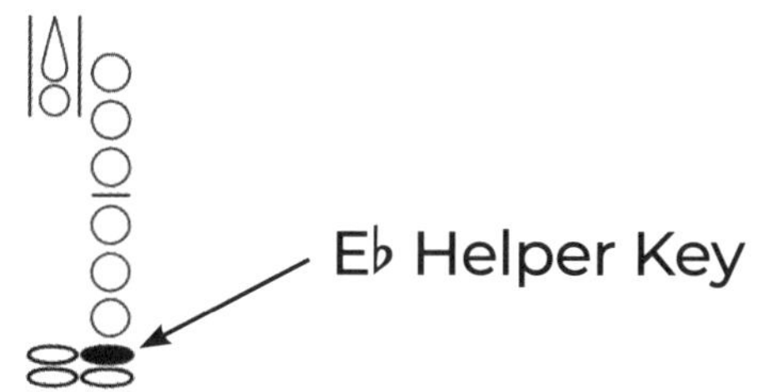


Practice the following warm-up every day before playing in the altissimo register.

## Stretching Our Limits

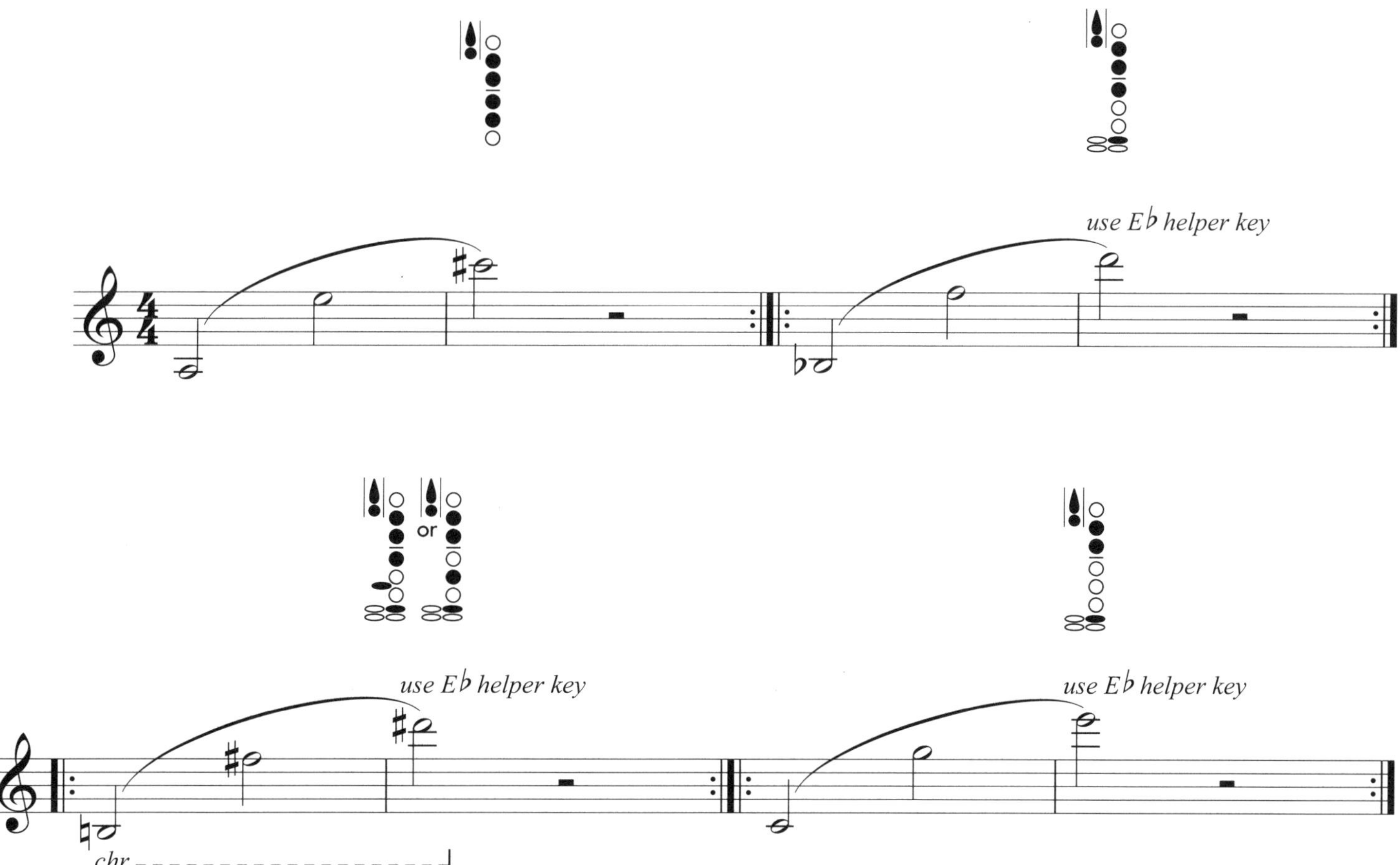

Loopy Loop Prep for Good Old Summertime

# IN THE GOOD OLE SUMMERTIME

Words by Ren Shields
Music by George Evans

**Waltz, in 1** 𝅗𝅥. **= 50**

## Loopy Loop Prep for Shenandoah

# SHENANDOAH

American Folksong

Andante

*mf* *f* *mf*

*f* *mf* *f*

*mf* *f*

*mp* *mp*

Loopy Loop Prep for My Bonnie

# MY BONNIE LIES OVER THE OCEAN

Traditional

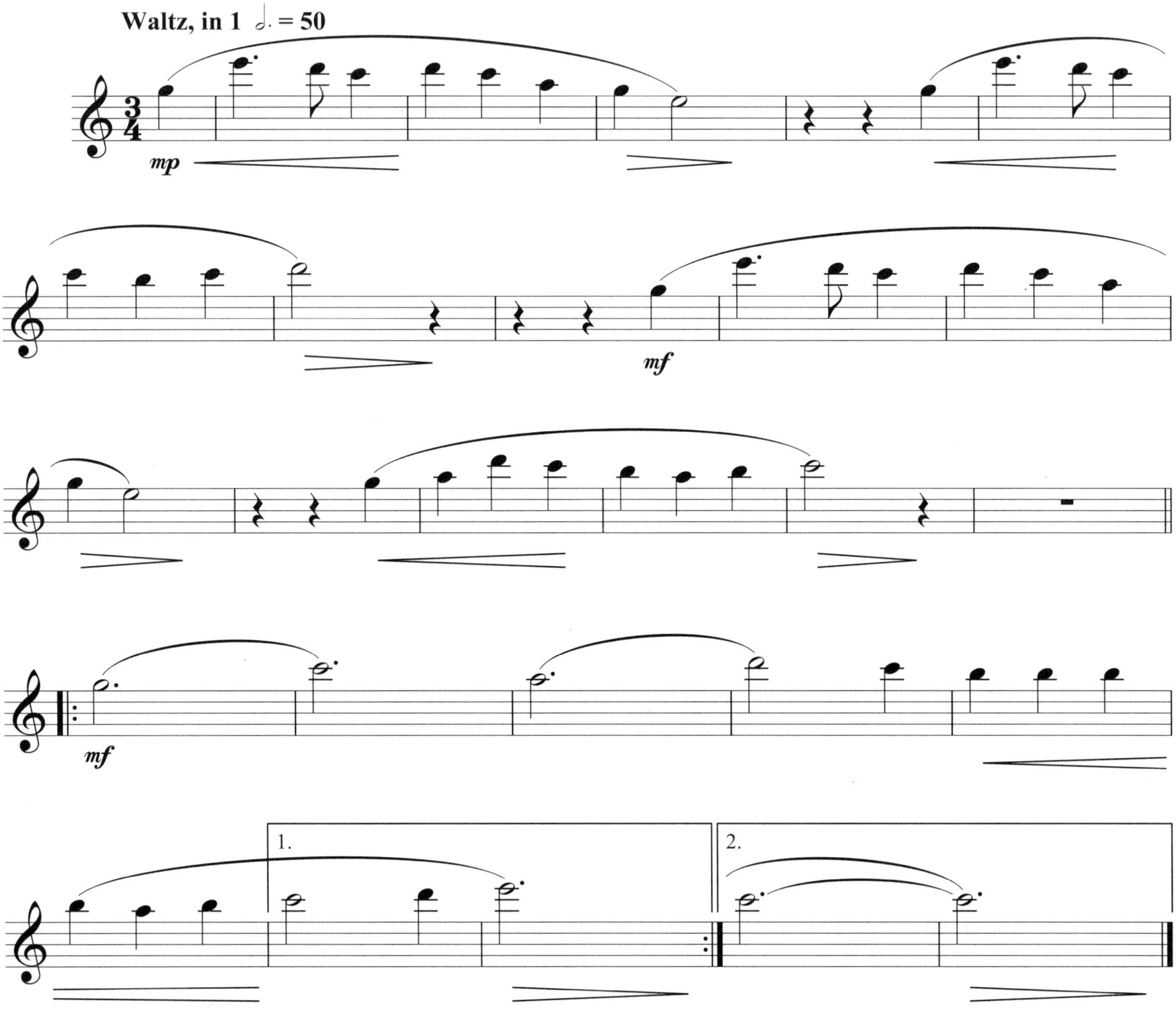

**Waltz, in 1** ♩. = 50

*mp*

*mf*

*mf*

1.

2.

# LET'S GO FLY A KITE

from MARY POPPINS

Words and Music by Richard M. Sherman and Robert B. Sherman

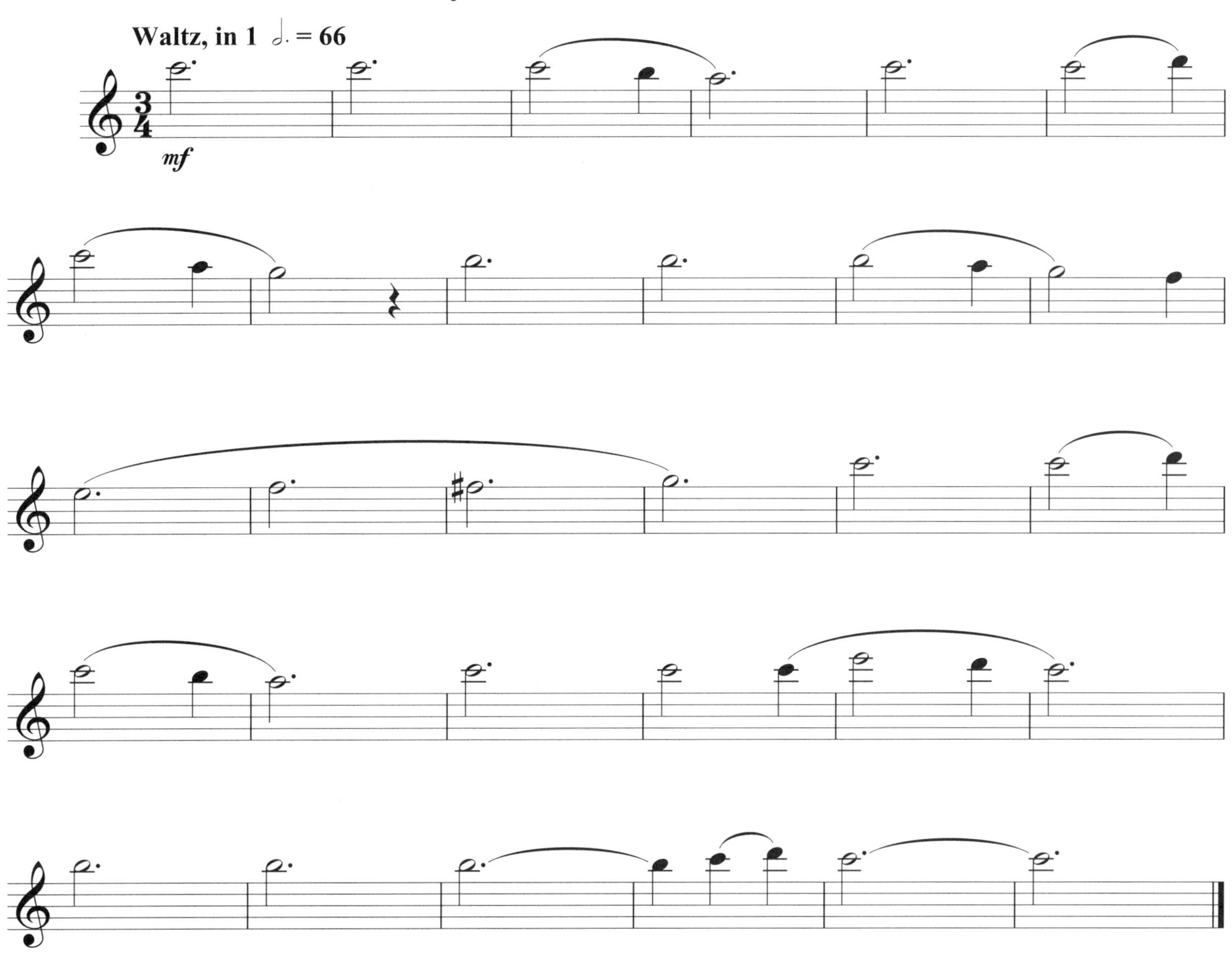

# HANUKKAH, O HANUKKAH

Traditional

## 6/8 Time

Remember, the bottom number of our time signature tells us what kind of note gets one beat. So far, we have seen a quarter note (4) and a half note (2) as the bottom number. When an 8 is on the bottom, an eighth note gets one beat. In 6/8 time, there are six eighth notes in a bar, and each one gets one beat. However, they are often grouped into two sets of three and are felt in two larger beats that we subdivide into three. We can think ONE two three FOUR five six.

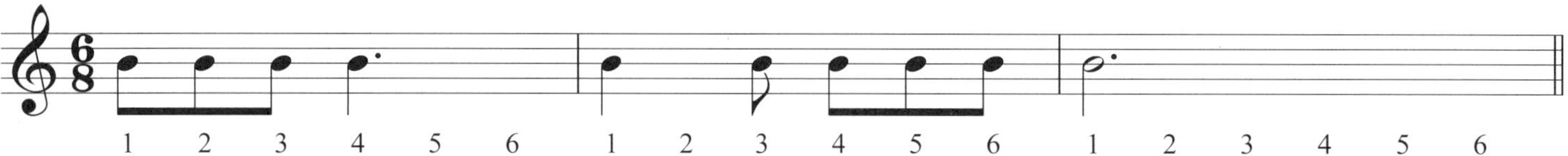

### Clapping Introducing 6/8 Time

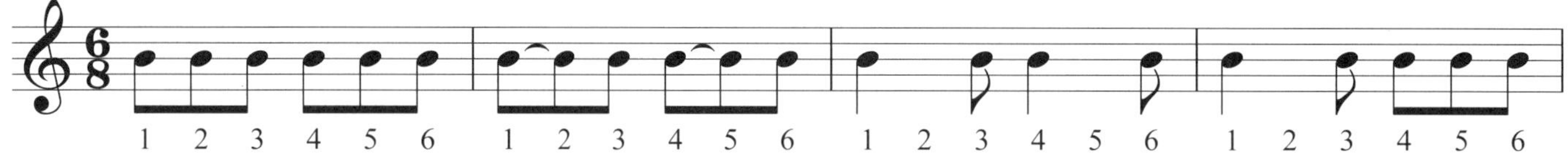


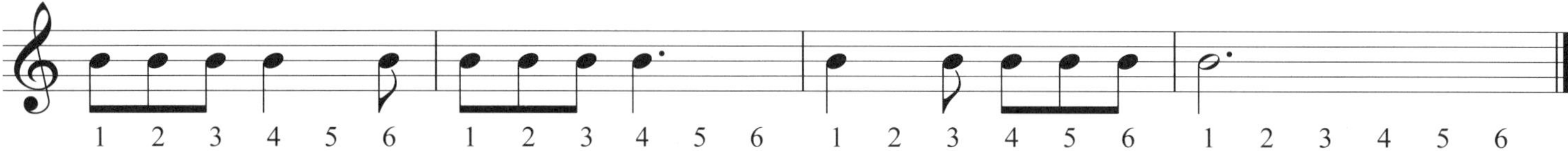

# THE MULBERRY BUSH

Traditional

# FOLLOW THE YELLOW BRICK ROAD/WE'RE OFF TO SEE THE WIZARD

from THE WIZARD OF OZ

Lyric by E.Y. "Yip" Harburg
Music by Harold Arlen

**Allegro**

**Follow the Yellow Brick Road**

*mp*

**We're Off to See the Wizard**

*f*

*f*

# WE ARE THE CHAMPIONS

Words and Music by Freddie Mercury

## Key of A-Flat

This key signature has four flats: B-flat, E-flat, A-flat, and D-flat.

# THE ANTS GO MARCHING IN

Traditional

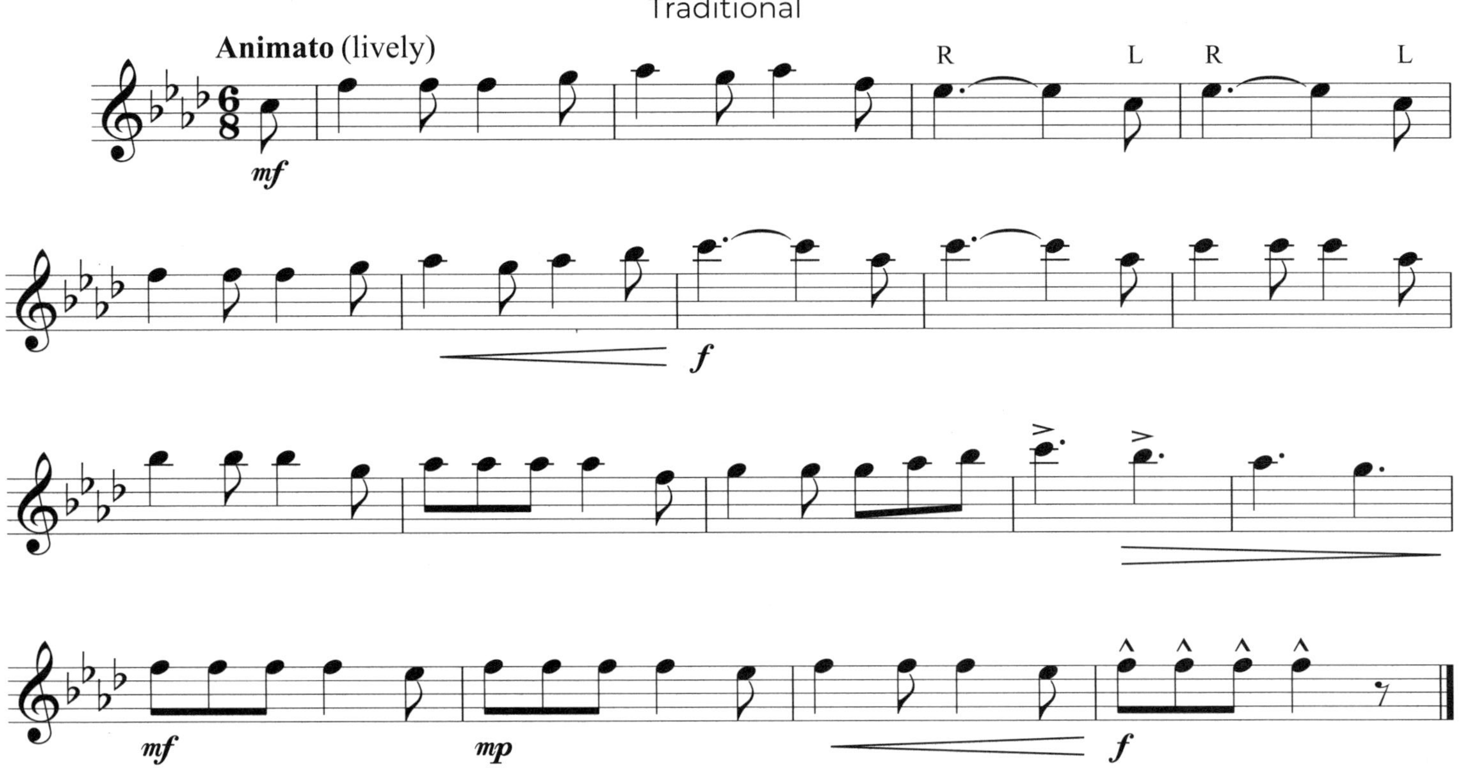

# NORWEGIAN WOOD (THIS BIRD HAS FLOWN)

Words and Music by John Lennon and Paul McCartney

## Clapping More 6/8 Time

# PERFECT

Words and Music by Ed Sheeran

# GLIMPSE OF US

Words and Music by Joji Kusunoki, Connor McDonough, Riley McDonough, Joel Castillo and Alexis Kesselman

# LIBERTY BELL MARCH

By John Philip Sousa

In "Rondo," you will hear 4 clicks (each representing three eighth notes, or two big beats per bar) before bar 1. If you are playing the top line, you'll need to place the pickup note before beat 1.

# DUET: RONDO

By Ignaz Pleyel

f
f
p

f
f

# LESSON 14:
# Continuing Your Journey

## Congratulations!

You have reached the last lesson in *Do-It-Yourself Clarinet*. In this lesson, you will find fun music to play in many styles, often in the original keys, so you can play along with recordings. We hope that you have enjoyed this musical journey and will carry on with some of the good clarinet habits that you have developed.

CLARINET TALK

**What does B♭ Clarinet mean?**
Musical instruments come in different keys. Any instrument that is not in "C" is called a transposing instrument. If an instrument is pitched in B♭, like most clarinets, it means that when you play a C, it sounds like a B♭ on the piano. This means you cannot play along with most other instruments while reading the same music (unless they are also B♭ instruments like the trumpet or tenor saxophone). A piano is an example of a non-transposing instrument, also referred to as either a "C instrument" or a "concert-pitched" instrument. If you are trying to play along with a piano, you need to play one note higher to match it. Published music for clarinet and piano is already transposed in the clarinet part by the publisher so that you can read it normally and match the piano part.

### Loopy Loops G Major Middle

TOOLBOX

**Rubato**

*Rubato* means to play very freely, which can allow the player to stretch or push the tempo expressively.

# DANNY BOY

Words by Frederick Edward Weatherly
Traditional Irish Folk Melody

f mp mf rit. p

# ASHOKAN FAREWELL

Theme from PBS Series THE CIVIL WAR

By Jay Ungar

# I SAY A LITTLE PRAYER*

Lyric by Hal David
Music by Burt Bacharach

*As sung by Dionne Warwick

# BABY ELEPHANT WALK

from the Paramount Picture HATARI!

Words by Hal David
Music by Henry Mancini

TOOLBOX

**5/4 Time**

**5** = Five beats in each measure
**4** = A quarter note receives one beat

5/4 time can be felt in quarter note groups of 3+2 or 2+3, depending on the feel of the song. In "Take Five" and "Mission: Impossible Theme," we can think ONE two three FOUR five.

# TAKE FIVE

By Paul Desmond

# MISSION: IMPOSSIBLE THEME

from the Paramount Television Series MISSION: IMPOSSIBLE

By Lalo Schifrin

**TOOLBOX**

**Tenutos Under Slurs**
When we see the tenuto mark (small line) on a slurred note, we want to think of stretching it and leaning on it just a little bit with our air. This gives it a very gentle emphasis.

# LA FILLE AUX CHEVEUX DE LIN (THE GIRL WITH THE FLAXEN HAIR)

By Claude Debussy

# AMERICA

from WEST SIDE STORY

Lyrics by Stephen Sondheim

Music by Leonard Bernstein

# MOONLIGHT SERENADE

Words by Mitchell Parish
Music by Glenn Miller

TOOLBOX

**Quarter-Note Triplets**

A quarter-note triplet is three equal notes in two beats. Clap or play the following example on your clarinet. In the first bar, it is all eighth-note triplets. In the second bar, there are ties in the second half. Imagine those notes are still separate to help you count. In the third bar, these tied notes are written as a quarter-note triplet, which is the same sound as the second bar.

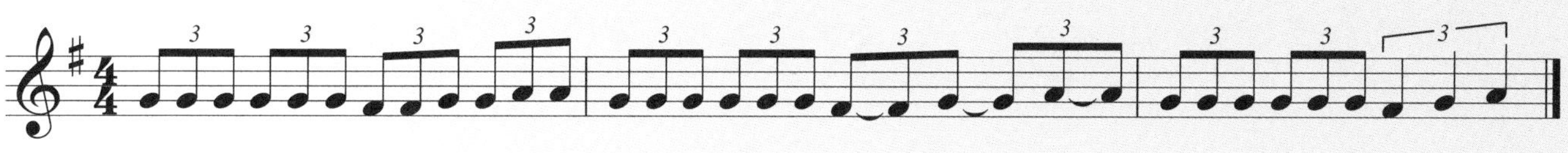

# DUET: WHAT A WONDERFUL WORLD

Words and Music by George David Weiss and Bob Thiele

Adagio ♩ = 72

mp mf mp mf mf mp

mf
mp
f
f

mf
mf
mf
f
f
f
mf
f

# APPENDIX A: Vocabulary Terms

**A tempo:** return to the original tempo

**Accelerando:** gradually speed up

**Accent:** an articulation, attack note by playing stronger

**Accidental:** sharp, flat, or natural that appears in a measure

**Adagio:** slow tempo, ♩ = 60-80

**Allegro:** fast tempo, ♩ = 120-156

**Andante:** slower "walking" tempo, ♩ = 80-108

**Articulation:** style in which you attack, or tongue each note

**Bar line:** divides the music staff into measures

**Breath mark:** indicates where to breathe

**Coda:** the conclusion

**Common time:** another way to notate 4/4

**Crescendo:** gradually get louder

**Cut time:** value of each beat from 4/4 is cut in half, also notated as 2/2

**Da Capo (D.C.):** from the beginning

**Dal Segno (D.S.):** from the sign

**Decrescendo:** gradually get softer

**Dot:** adds half of the value of the note

**Double bar:** indicates a new section within the music

**Dynamics:** indicate how loud or soft to play

**Embouchure:** position of mouth on the mouth piece

**Enharmonic:** two notes with the same pitch but written with different note names

**Fermata:** hold for a longer, unspecified time

**Fine:** the end

**Flat:** lowers note a half step

**Forte:** loud

**Fortissimo:** very loud

**Forward repeat:** repeat sign at the beginning of a measure

**Giocoso:** played in a very happy, lively style

**Interval:** distance between notes

**Key signature:** indicates whether to play the notes sharp, flat, or natural

**Largo:** very slow tempo, ♩ = 40-60

**Ledger lines:** lines that extend the music staff

**Marcato:** an articulation, with a strong attack and separation between notes

**Measure:** space between two bar lines

**Meter:** a regular recurring pattern of beats; time signature

**Metronome:** device used to keep a steady tempo

**Mezzo forte:** medium loud

**Mezzo piano:** medium soft

**Moderato:** medium tempo, ♩ = 108-120

**Natural:** cancels sharps or flats to return note back to its normal state

**Octave:** interval that is eight notes apart, both notes have the same name

**Phrase:** musical sentence, or complete idea

**Piano:** soft

**Pickup note:** note or group of notes that occur before the first full measure

**Presto:** very, very fast, ♩ = 176 and up

**Ritardando:** gradually slow down

**Sharp:** raises note a half step

**Shuffle:** a bluesy swing style

**Slur:** an articulation, connects two or more notes of any pitch

**Staccato:** an articulation, light and separated

**Staff:** lines and spaces where music is written

**Subdivision:** breaking the beat into smaller, even pieces

**Swing:** musical style where eighth notes are not even in length

**Syncopation:** rhythmic change where emphaisis shifts to the offbeat

**Tempo:** speed of the music

**Tenuto:** an articulation, note is held full value

**Tie:** connects two or more notes of the same pitch together

**Time signature:** indicates number of beats in a measure as well as which type of note receives one beat

**Treble clef:** also known as G clef; the clef used for clarinet players

**Trill:** rapidly moving back and forth between two notes that are next to each other

**Triplet:** three notes of equal length grouped together

**Vivace:** very fast, ♩ = 156-176

# APPENDIX B:
## Clarinet Fingerings

If you prefer to see these fingerings with photos of hands on a clarinet, refer to our digital Photo Fingering Chart in MyLibrary.

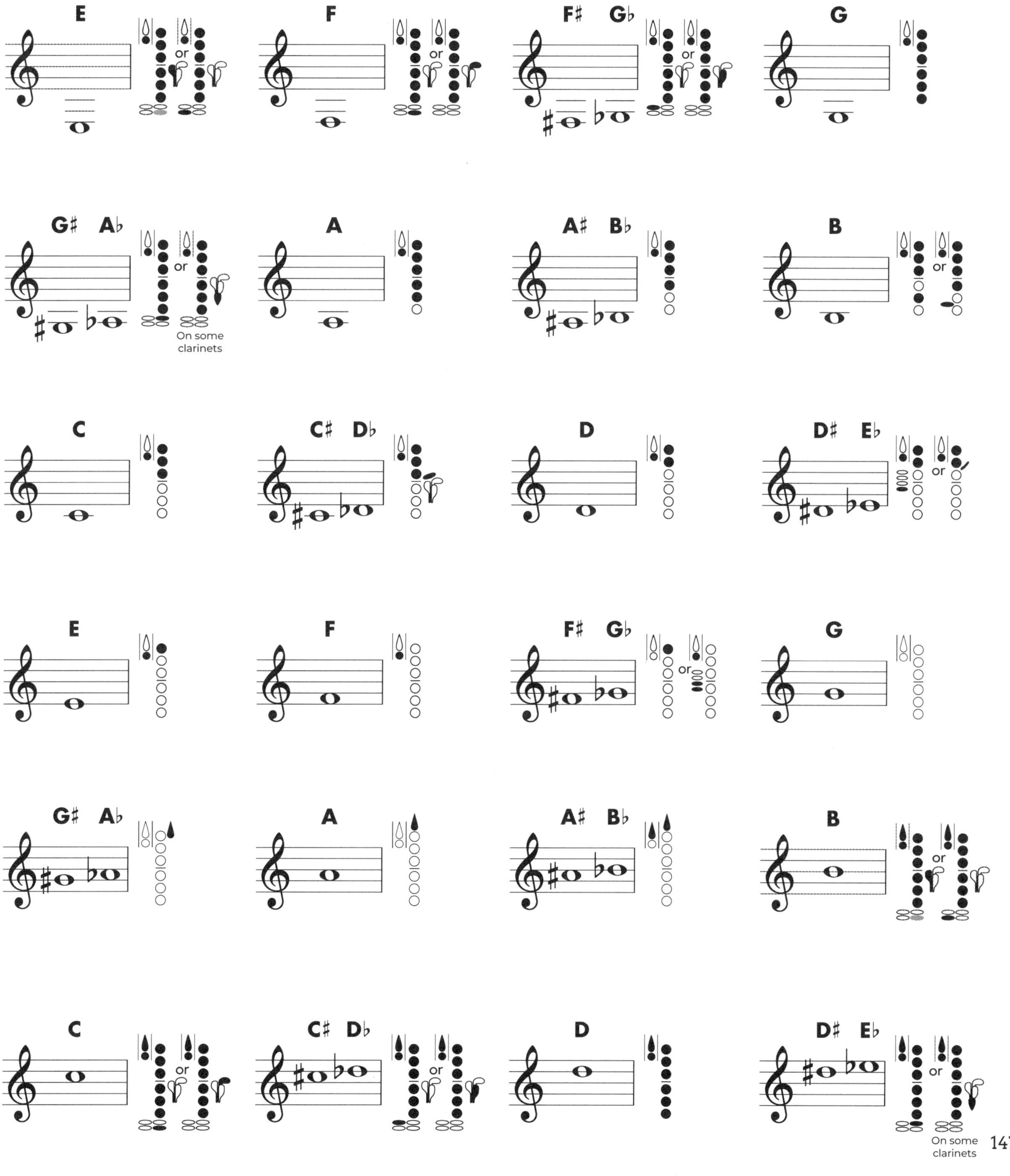

E
or
F
or
F♯ G♭
or
G
G♯ A♭
or
On some clarinets
A
A♯ B♭
B
or
C
C♯ D♭
D
D♯ E♭
or
E
F
F♯ G♭
or
G
G♯ A♭
A
A♯ B♭
B
or
C
or
C♯ D♭
or
D
D♯ E♭
or
On some clarinets

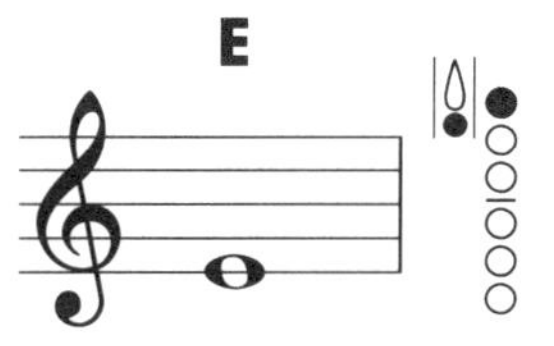

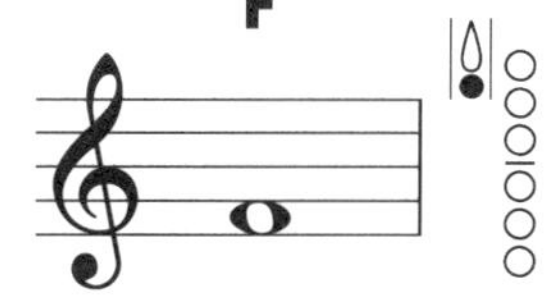

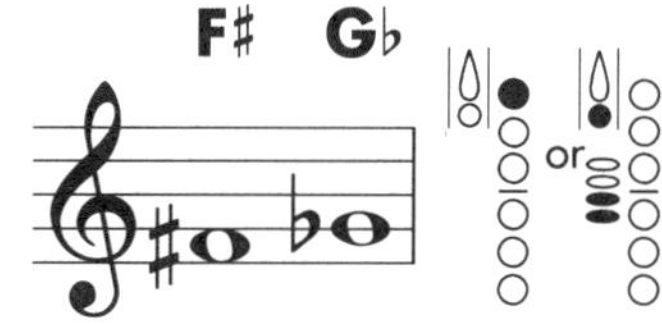

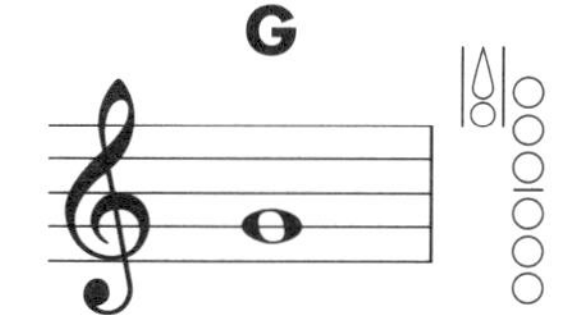

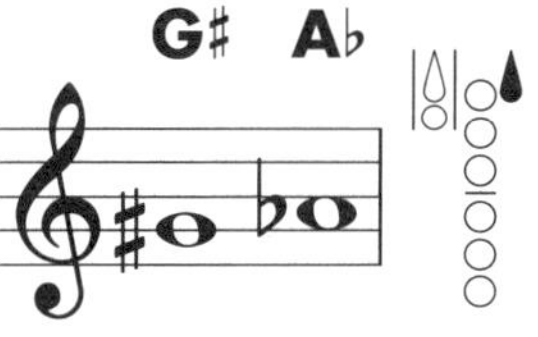

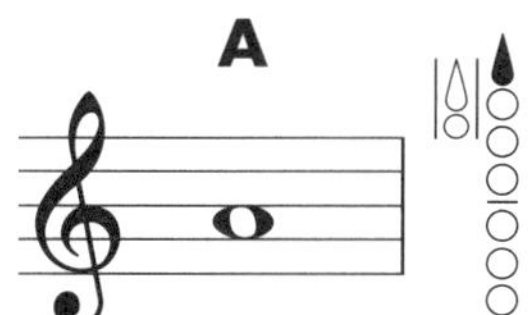

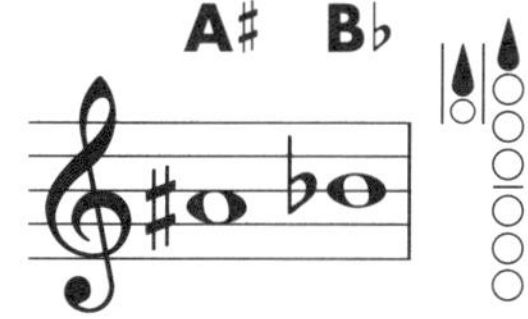

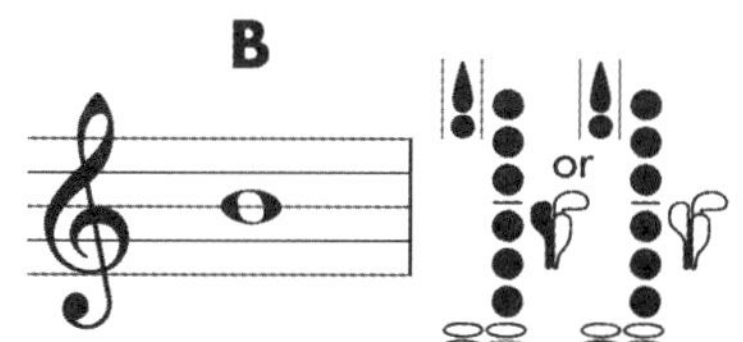

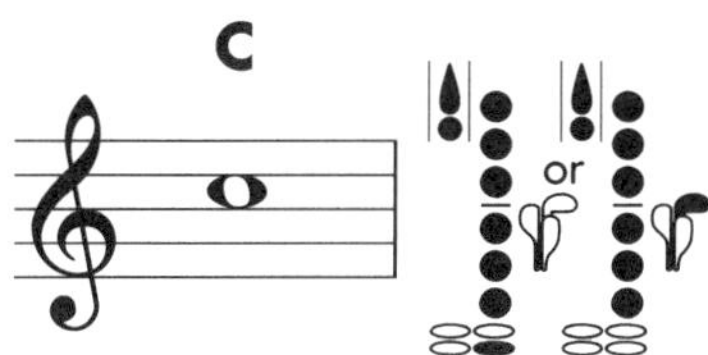

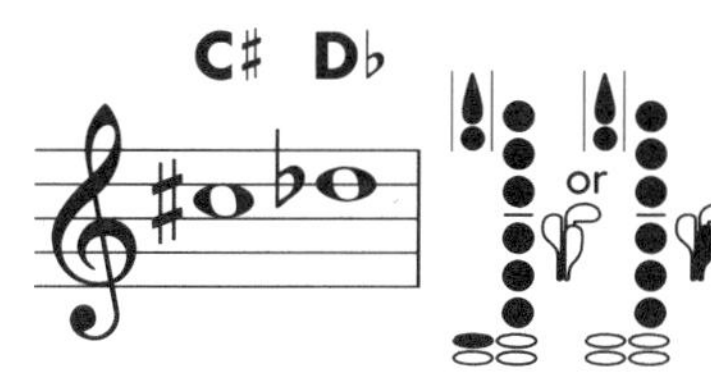

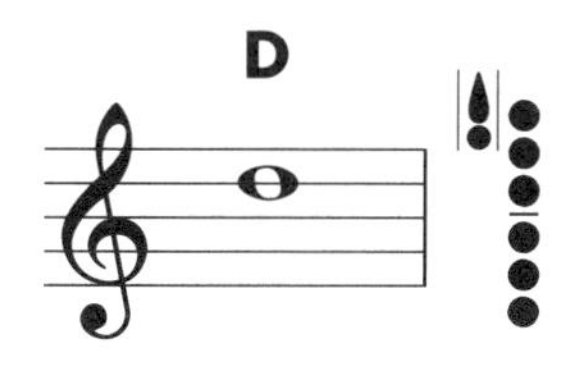

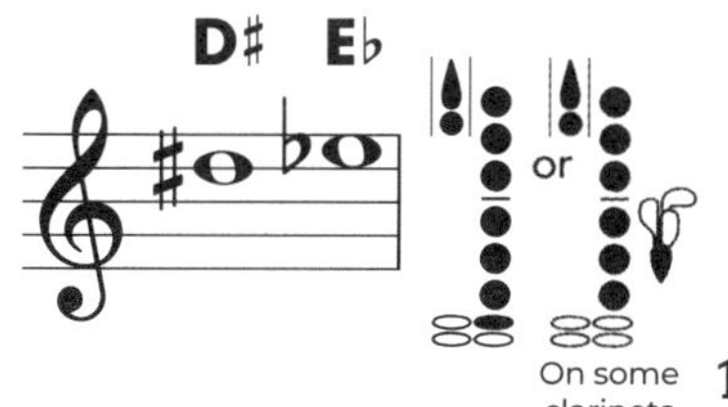

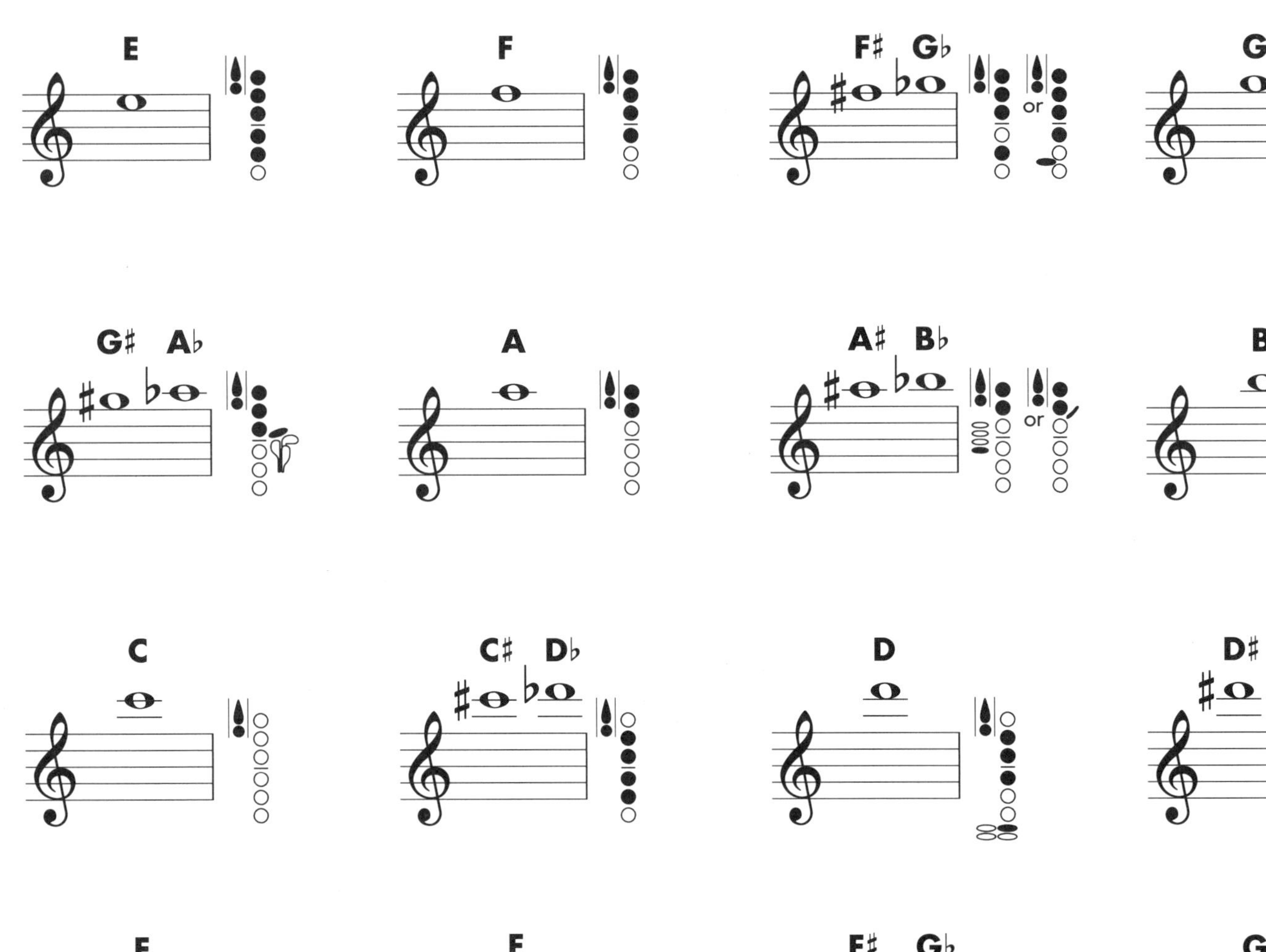
E
F
F♯ G♭
or
G
G♯ A♭
A
A♯ B♭
or
B
C
C♯ D♭
D
D♯ E♭
or
E
F
F♯ G♭
G